JAMES WATSON & FRANCIS CRICK: Discovery of the Double Helix and Beyond

Makers of Modern Science

JAMES WATSON & FRANCIS CRICK: Discovery of the Double Helix and Beyond

David E. Newton

Facts On File
New York

JAMES WATSON AND FRANCIS CRICK: Discovery of the Double Helix and Beyond

Copyright © 1992 by Instructional Horizons, Inc.

Facts On File, Inc.
460 Park Avenue South
New York NY 10016
USA

Library of Congress Cataloging-in-Publication Data
Newton, David E.
James Watson and Francis Crick : discovery of the double helix and beyond / David E. Newton.
    p. cm.—(Makers of modern science)
    Includes bibliographical references and index
    Summary: Presents biographies of the scientists who discovered the structure of the DNA molecule.
    ISBN 0-8160-2558-4
    1. DNA—Research—Juvenile literature. 2. Watson, James D., 1928– —Juvenile literature. 3. Crick, Francis, 1916– —Juvenile literature. 4. Molecular biologists—Biography—Juvenile literature. [1. Watson, James D., 1928– . 2. Crick, Francis, 1916– . 3. Molecular biologists. 4. DNA.] I. Title. II. Series
QP620.N49 1992
574.87'3282'0922—dc20
[B]   91-36544

A British CIP catalogue record for this book is available on request from the British Library.

Text design by Ron Monteleone
Jacket design by Catherine Hyman
Composition by Facts On File, Inc.
Manufactured by R. R. Donnelley & Sons
Printed in the United States of America

10 9 8 7 6 5 4 3 2 1

This book is printed on acid-free paper.

To Dr. John D'Emilio
with appreciation for his years of
friendship and professional inspiration

CONTENTS

INTRODUCTION: SPIRITS AND MOLECULES—WHAT IS LIFE?

This book is a detective story. It tells about one of the most difficult, most intriguing, and most important scientific discoveries of the 20th century.

Two scientists from very different backgrounds, one British and one American, worked together to discover how molecules in living bodies determine biological traits. These molecules tell a plant what type of leaves to grow, a deer when to shed its antlers, and a girl when to turn into a young woman. These molecules also provide a way of passing along this information from one generation to the next.

To better explain how this discovery will affect your life now and in the future, we will start with two stories about the way humans think about an important event in life: disease.

It is 1865. The Japanese warrior has taken ill with measles. His doctor is treating him with herbs to make him feel better. But both doctor and warrior know the cause of the disease—one of the warrior's enemies has hired a witch to cast a spell on the warrior. The witch has sent evil spirits into the warrior's body, causing measles.

The doctor's herbs will have no effect on the spirits. Another witch will have to be hired. This witch can call the evil spirits out of the warrior's body and make him well.

It is 1991. The young patient suffers from a rare condition known as severe immune deficiency disorder (SIDD). Her body is unable to fight any kind of infection. If she catches the measles, her body is completely unable to fight back. She may die from the disease.

A "vitalistic" theory of disease. This early 20th-century Japanese print shows a samurai warrior armed to prevent an attack of measles. The figures in the background may represent a wizard attempting to cast a spell on the warrior.   (National Institutes of Health)

Health problems that are an annoyance to her friends, relatives, and neighbors can kill her. As a result, she must live inside a large plastic bubble that keeps out all germs.

The patient's doctors think her illness is caused by the absence of a particular kind of molecule in the girl's body. They think they have a way to correct the problem. They will inject her with a substance that will force her body to start making the missing molecule. If the treatment works, the girl's body will become healthy.

These stories describe two very different ways of treating disease. The first tells how a 19th-century Japanese doctor tried to cure measles. The doctor believed that herbs and drugs could be used to treat some kinds of illness. But he knew that other kinds of disease were beyond his power to deal with. He was convinced that spirits could enter the human body and cause problems. Witch doctors, sorcerers, and magicians had to be called to treat problems like these.

Many people in the 1990s hold the same beliefs. Black magic and Voodoo are both based on such beliefs. Christian Scientists hold similar beliefs. They think that illness can be cured by praying to God, rather than by taking medicines.

These beliefs spring from a philosophy known as *vitalism*. The theory of vitalism teaches that living things are basically different from nonliving things. Anything that is alive consists of more than just atoms and molecules. It also contains a special quality that is beyond human control and that scientists can not analyze. That special quality has been called by names such as "spirit" (or "spirits"), "the breath of God," "a vital flame," or "the spark of life."

The philosophy of vitalism is widespread, even among people who do not believe in Voodoo or Christian Science. For example, about once a year, some reporter will write a story about the value of the chemicals found in the human body. The story will explain that the body contains about 3 grams of iron, worth 3 cents at today's prices, 35 grams of magnesium, worth about $1.50, 0.1 gram of copper, worth less than a penny, and so on. Based on these calculations, the chemicals in a human body might be valued at much less than $100.

These stories sometimes conclude with the observation that human bodies are more than just a collection of chemicals. How many people believe that a scientist could ever start with a bunch of chemicals and make a living body? After all, the reporter might point out, "life" is more than just a collection of atoms and molecules. A scientist might be able to manufacture all the molecules found in a living organism. But he or she could never provide that "spark" or "breath of life" that makes living things different from nonliving things.

The second story above is based on a very different assumption. That assumption is that living things are not special in any way. They are basically no different from rocks, minerals, and other nonliving objects. Plants and animals are more complicated than most nonliving things, to be sure. But they are made of atoms and molecules that are the same as, or similar to, those found in nonliving things. Furthermore, the same laws of chemistry and physics that apply to rainstorms, machines, and erosion also apply to things that are alive.

This view of living things is known as *reductionism*. The term suggests that the composition and properties of even the most complex of living organisms can be reduced to the simplest forms of matter, atoms, and molecules.

Thus, health and disease can be understood by using our knowledge of science. There is no need to call upon spirits, gods, or other supernatural beings for cures.

Perhaps this difference of opinion sounds as if it belongs in a philosophy class. But it has some very important significance in our everyday lives. First, if living plants and animals are nothing other than atoms and molecules that obey the laws of chemistry and physics, then scientists can eventually know all there is to know about health and disease, about life and death. We do not have to call upon magic, mysticism, and spirits to solve the great events of life.

Second, if death and disease can be treated purely by scientific methods, then so can every other aspect of human life. If scientists can cure disease by injecting new molecules into a person, why can they not make other changes in a healthy person's body? What is to prevent a scientist from changing the chemical structure of a person's body to make that person taller or shorter, more or less intelligent, blond- or red-haired, witty or dull . . . and so on?

Some writers have worried about this possibility for centuries. They have warned about scientists who wanted and were able to make humans with any characteristics they chose. These concerns have lead to some of the greatest of all science fiction stories, such as *Frankenstein* and *The Boys from Brazil*.

But these stories remain science *fiction* only so long as you believe that there is something special about life that scientists can not create or manipulate. If the theory of vitalism is wrong, scientists do have the potential for changing life in any way they choose. It may be decades or centuries before they know all they need to know to make those changes. But there is nothing to prevent that day from coming eventually.

A crucial piece in the puzzle about the nature of life is the connection between atoms and molecules and living things, the connection between chemistry and physics and biology. Can a person's red hair or green eyes or some aspects of intelligence be explained in terms of specific atoms and molecules in that person's body?

Today we know that the answer to that question is yes. Scientists now know that eye and hair color, disease, and many other attributes of human life can be described in terms of specific molecules found in the body.

Probably the most important breakthrough in reaching this point was the discovery of the structure of one specific kind of molecule, the DNA molecule. That discovery was made by James Watson and Francis Crick in 1953. Some scientists have called this discovery one of the two or three greatest accomplishments in the history of science.

Who are James Dewey Watson and Francis Harry Compton Crick? How did they become involved in a study of the molecules of life? What is the story of their discovery? What have their lives been like since this great accomplishment? These are the questions that we attempt to answer in the rest of this book.

1

FRANCIS CRICK: THE EARLY YEARS

Sunday mornings may not have been Francis Crick's favorite time of the week. As son of the local church secretary, he obviously had to attend services at Northampton Congregational Church. But there were many other things a bright, curious young man like Francis would have preferred doing to sitting in a church pew.

In fact, Crick expressed this view later in life. He wrote that his required church attendance probably contributed to the anti-vitalist philosophy that has so dominated his thought and work as an adult.

Francis's opposition to religion was a break from family tradition. So was much else in his life. He was born into a family of traditional, middle-class businessmen in Northampton, England, on June 8, 1916. His grandfather, Walter Drawbridge Crick, had been director of a boot and shoe factory, Latimer Crick and Company. Although he lived to be only 46 years old, grandfather Crick amassed a small fortune at the factory. When he died in 1903, management of the business passed to Francis's uncle Walter. Later, Francis's father, Harry, joined Walter at the boot and shoe factory.

Unfortunately, the years following World War I were difficult times for many English businesses. The Crick boot and shoe company was one of thousands that failed in the postwar period. When the business collapsed, Uncle Walter moved to the United States. For the last 18 years of his life, he was a sales agent for various shoe companies there.

Francis's father decided to move his family to London. There he managed a series of shoe shops. Although the shops provided the Cricks with a decent living, they did not restore the fortune lost in the collapse of the boot and shoe factory.

One reason for the move to London was the educational opportunities it provided the Crick boys, Francis and Anthony. The men of the Crick family had all attended Mill Hill School in London as live-in students. Francis himself had graduated from Mill Hill in 1934.

He was remembered by the school's headmaster, Michael Hart, as a "highly competent" student who was "expected to do very well." Hart also recalled some of the personal characteristics—his high, shrill voice and laughter and talkativeness, for example—for which Francis was to be known throughout his life. But, Hart also noted, no one at Mill Hill had the least notion that young Francis would have as brilliant a career as he eventually did.

The move to London by the Crick family made it possible for Anthony to continue the Mill Hill tradition, but as a day-student. At the same time, Francis was able to commute to his new school, University College in London.

The one passion in young Francis's life was science. He earned distinction in physics and math and did well in chemistry at Mill Hill. But much of his early learning in science was self-taught. No one else in the family had much background or interest in the subject. When young Francis showed a constant, singleminded attention to anything scientific, the family decided he must have gone "crackers" on the subject.

By the time Francis reached college, everyone assumed that science would be his career and that he would do well in it. There was some disappointment, then, when he was graduated from University College in 1937 with "only" a good "second" in physics.

After receiving his bachelor of science degree at University College, he stayed on to do graduate work in physics. The topic of his graduate study was the viscosity of water (that is, how easily water flows) at high temperatures. His work was nearly completed two years later when World War II broke out. Crick left London and joined the Admiralty Research Laboratory at Teddington.

At Teddington, Crick was assigned to do research on the design of better mines for the English navy. Scientists at the laboratory were trying to find ways to make mines that could "outsmart" the anti-mine devices invented by the Germans. Whenever the Germans found a way to detect and destroy one type of English mine, the laboratory came up with a new type.

(In an odd twist of fate, Crick's research project back at University College was destroyed by a German mine, dropped as a bomb, in the early years of the war.)

One of Crick's biographers, Robert Olby, describes a case in which Crick was assigned a specific mine problem to solve. He almost immediately saw a simple and direct solution. The solution had escaped other members of the research team. Olby cites this incident as an example of Crick's brilliant ability to see through complex, difficult problems and come up with clever, innovative solutions.

Olby also points out that Crick was not especially diplomatic when working with his peers. He had a tendency to make his ideas known directly, without much concern that he might offend others' feelings. As a result, Olby says, there were "frequent tensions" at Teddington, and Crick's superior officer often "found himself soothing officers hurt when Crick had told them they were talking nonsense."

The end of the war presented Crick with new choices. At first, he decided to stay with the Admiralty and was assigned to the Naval Intelligence Division in London. His plans were to do basic research in either particle physics or physics as it applies to living systems.

But gradually his interest shifted in a new direction: to the field of biology. That choice may seem surprising. After all, Crick had nearly finished his work on a doctorate in physics before the war. Physics and biology are both sciences, of course, but they are very different in many ways. Physics deals with some of the most difficult, abstract concepts in all of science, those involving energy. Biology is concerned with the study of concrete, living organisms. Many scientists in the 1940s would have seen little connection between these two branches of science.

Crick claims that he chose biology as his new career for two reasons. First, he was an atheist who wanted to see religious ideas chased out of science. An atheist is a person who does not believe in the existence of God. Not that scientists consciously allowed religious beliefs to determine the way they did scientific research, but since the earliest days of science, religious ideas had subtly influenced scientific thinking. An example was the 18th-century theory of vitalism.

According to the vitalistic theory, chemicals found in living organisms were thought to be fundamentally different from those in nonliving materials. The citric acid, tartaric acid, and sucrose found in fruits, for example, were thought to be different in some basic way from the salt, gypsum, and silicon dioxide found in rocks. The "living" chemicals were thought to contain a "vital spirit" that had been breathed into them by God. As a result, scientists who held this theory believed that the methods used to study living things had to be different from the methods used to study nonliving materials.

By the 1940s, scientists no longer believed in the vitalistic theory. Yet, it was not difficult to show how those older ideas still influenced scientific thought. For example, many biologists believed that "life" was more than a collection of chemicals. To be sure, it was possible to analyze a living organism into certain specific chemical compounds. But few biologists were willing to imagine that any scientist could simply put those chemicals together and produce a living being. "Life" was thought to be more than the sum of its parts. An additional "nudge" was needed to get those compounds acting together as a living organism. Biologists no longer called that nudge the "breath of God," but that might have been close to what they had in mind.

Crick was eager to rid scientific thinking of this "mystical" influence. He believed that all forms of matter—both living and nonliving—could be analyzed and understood in terms of chemistry and physics. Living materials might be more complex and more difficult to understand. But that did not mean that they required special methods of study.

And who better to apply this philosophy of biological study than Crick himself? He already had an extensive background in physics. All he needed to do now was to become an expert in chemistry and biology also!

The second influence on Crick's decision was a book by Erwin Schrodinger, *What Is Life?* Schrodinger was a brilliant Austrian physicist who in 1926 had developed an important model of the atom, the smallest division of an element that retains all the properties of that element. Schrodinger's book reflected much of Crick's own thinking, namely that life can be understood by means of physical and chemical principles. Crick was convinced that Schrodinger's ideas would soon lead to an exciting new line of research, one in which chemistry and physics would be used to explain life. And Crick wanted to be in on the ground floor in this research.

Thus, in the spring of 1947, Crick applied for a student research grant from the English Medical Research Council. In that application, he outlined his new research interests:

> *The particular field which excites my interest is the division between the living and the nonliving, as typified by, say proteins, viruses, bacteria, and the structure of chromosomes. The eventual goal, which is somewhat remote, is the description of these activities in terms of their structure, i.e., the spatial distribution of their constituent atoms, in so far as this may prove possible. This might be called the chemical physics of biology.*

By the fall of 1947, Crick had taken the first steps toward his new career. He began research at the Strangeways Laboratories at Cambridge University. That research involved a study of cells. Crick used a traditional biological approach, with little or no effort to use chemistry or physics in his research. This was not the revolutionary new approach to biology about which he had been dreaming.

Before long, however, he heard of an opportunity to go in just that direction. Also working at Cambridge was a group of scientists studying the structure of proteins. Leader of the group was Max Perutz, an Austrian chemist. Perutz's specialty was X-ray crystallography

X-ray crystallography is a method of analyzing the fundamental structure of materials. The technique uses X rays, instead of light, to take pictures of a material at the atomic level. X-ray crystallography was developed in the early 1900s by Sir William Henry Bragg and his son, William Lawrence. In 1947, the younger Bragg

Max Perutz in 1980. (Medical Research Council, Laboratory of Molecular Biology, copyrighted by Cambridge Evening News)

was director of the Cavendish Laboratory at which the Perutz group was working.

X-ray crystallography can be used with any material that will crystallize. During crystallization, the atoms in the material arrange themselves in a regular, orderly pattern. When X rays are shined on the crystal, they are deflected by the atoms. The deflected X rays produce a pattern that corresponds to the arrangement of atoms in the crystal. This pattern is captured on a photographic plate, resulting in a picture of the atomic structure of the material. The photograph on page 7 shows the kind of photograph produced by X-ray crystallography.

The problem for the X-ray crystallographer is to figure out what the X-ray photograph tells about the material—that is, what arrangement of atoms in the material will account for the pattern revealed in the photograph. Very sophisticated mathematical techniques had to be developed to help answer that question.

By the mid-1950s, X-ray crystallography was a standard, relatively straightforward method for studying minerals, which often have a relatively simply crystal structure. The technique could also be used with large, complex molecules, like those that make up living systems.

For example, in 1950 it was about the only good method available for studying protein structure. Proteins are among the largest, most complex of all molecules. They play a number of critical roles in living organisms. They are the building materials of which all cells are made. In the form of hormones, they carry chemical

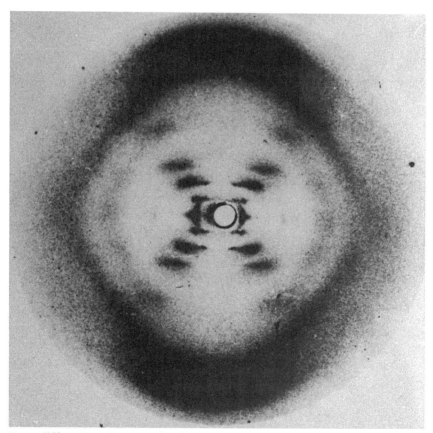

X-ray diffraction photograph of a DNA molecule. (Cold Spring Harbor Laboratory)

messages from one part of the body to another. As enzymes, they make possible the vast majority of chemical reactions that occur in the body. It was obvious to scientists that understanding the nature of proteins was crucial to understanding the nature of life itself.

But X-ray crystallography of large molecules presents some special problems. First, getting those molecules to crystallize was often difficult. Second, the photographs of complex molecules often presented pictures that were blurred and unclear. Finally, even the clearest photographs were usually very difficult to analyze and interpret.

In spite of these problems, Crick was eager to join Perutz's group. It seemed to be doing exactly the kind of research in which he was interested. The researchers in Perutz's group were looking for the connection between *physical structure* (the shape of the protein molecule) and its *biological function* (the job the protein had to do in an organism). Moreover, the Perutz group was working on one of the most basic questions of all, the physical and chemical basis of heredity.

For nearly a half century, scientists had explained heredity by using the concept of "genes." The Austrian monk Gregor Mendel had conducted basic research on heredity in the mid-1800s. Mendel was able to develop a few basic laws that described his results. Those laws could best be stated, Mendel found, by assuming the existence of certain "packages" of information later called genes. No one, including Mendel, knew exactly what genes were. They were simply an idea that helped describe how traits are passed from one generation to the next.

At about the same time that Mendel was discovering the laws of heredity, a second line of genetic research was going on in another field of science, chemistry. Chemists were looking for specific compounds that might be able to transmit hereditary characteristics. The most promising candidates for this role seemed to be proteins.

Proteins appeared to be the logical choice as "genetic molecules" because there are literally thousands of genetic characteristics that can be transmitted from one individual to another and from one generation to the next. Examples in humans include hair color, eye color, skin color, and handedness. Any family of compounds that can carry such a huge variety of different messages would have to be made of very complex molecules. And about the most complex molecules known to chemists at the time were proteins.

The argument was that one type of protein might carry the genetic message for red hair, another type of protein might carry the message for blonde hair, a third type of protein might carry the message for black hair, and so on.

This theory required that there be millions and millions of different types of protein molecules, each capable of transmitting a particular genetic characteristic. But that seemed to be no problem. By one calculation, at least 24×10^{17} (that is, 24 followed by 17 zeroes) different types of protein molecules can exist. That much diversity among proteins seemed to make them a logical choice for the "genetic molecules" for which chemists were searching.

By the late 1930s, scientists were convinced that genes were some kind of protein molecules. The problem was that no one had any idea how proteins might store genetic information nor how the information could be passed from parents to offspring. The solutions to these problems would constitute an enormous breakthrough in biology. They would give scientists a specific, concrete way to understand how heredity occurs, using the principles of chemistry and physics. So the study of proteins by Perutz's group was precisely the kind of research for which Crick had been looking.

In 1949 Crick transferred from the Strangeways Laboratory to the Cavendish Laboratory at Cambridge. In making this transfer, he also abandoned the biology-oriented research of the previous two years for the physical-oriented research of the Perutz group.

At the same time, Crick asked permission to register as a doctoral student at Gonville and Caius College at Cambridge. He was certainly not a typical doctoral student. He was 33 years old and had recently married for a second time, to the former Odile Speed. Nonetheless, he was given permission to enter the doctoral program at Gonville and Caius.

In his first year at the Cavendish, Crick devoted himself to mastering a subject about which he had previously known nothing, protein X-ray crystallography. At the end of that year, he presented his first seminar to the Perutz group. At the suggestion of another member of the Perutz group, John Kendrew, Crick titled his talk, "What Mad Pursuit."

In his 20-minute talk, Crick essentially told the senior members of the research team—Perutz, Bragg, and Kendrew—that both the methods they had been using and the conclusions they had reached were wrong. Moreover, Crick presented his views in such an insistent manner that he "drove Bragg [his boss] off the deep end."

This was not a very promising beginning for this brash young man from Northampton. The main thing that saved him from a disastrous early end to his Cavendish career was that he was completely right in his critique, and everyone on the team soon realized it.

CHAPTER 1 NOTES

p. 3   "found himself soothing . . ." Robert Olby, "Francis Crick, DNA, and the Central Dogma," *Daedalus* (Fall 1970): p. 941.

p. 5   "The particular field . . ." As cited in Horace Freeland Judson, *The Eighth Day of Creation* (New York: Simon and Schuster, 1979), p. 109.

p. 10   "drove Bragg . . ." Judson, *The Eighth Day*, p. 110.

2
JAMES WATSON: THE EARLY YEARS

The headmaster at Francis Crick's school has said that no one at the Mill Hill School had any "real expectations of his future brilliance." The principal at James Watson's high school could hardly have made the same remark.

Watson's powerful intellect was obvious early in his life. He graduated from high school at the age of 15 and immediately entered the University of Chicago. Four years later he was graduated from Chicago with bachelor of philosophy and bachelor of science degrees.

One of his teachers at Chicago says that Watson "must have been very keen" because he had given him two A's and "I don't give very many A's." Another instructor, the famous biologist Paul Weiss, recalled that "he never took any notes and yet at the end of the course he came top of the class."

Like Crick, Watson grew up in an average, working-class family. His father, James Dewey Watson, was a businessman who worked for a correspondence school. Watson remembers that "it was an awful job. He would have been better as a schoolteacher, but he never ended up that way."

His mother, Jean (Mitchell) Watson, was employed as a secretary at the University of Chicago. She also did volunteer work for the Democratic Party and held party meetings in the basement of the Watson home. His father belonged to the Episcopalian church, and his mother was a Catholic. But neither seemed to have very strong religious commitments.

When James was born on April 6, 1928, the family was living on Chicago's South Side, "between the steel mills and the university," but, he points out, "slightly closer to the mills." He has been described as a "tall and skinny and uncoordinated" young man with unusually sharp mental abilities. He discovered at an early age that two things at which he was very good were reading and learning facts.

It was the latter skill that led to the first notable accomplishment of his young life. At the age of 12 he was selected as a member of the Quiz Kids.

The Quiz Kids radio program was first heard on NBC radio in June 1940. Each week, five children between the ages of 5 and 16 were bombarded with questions that would stump most adults. For their efforts, the young contestants each received a $100 savings bond. The top three scorers on each program were invited back the following week.

James appeared on the Quiz Kids program three times. Then he lost his place on the show because he could not answer questions on Shakespeare and the Old Testament. "If I had known the religious questions," Watson later said, "my father would have been angry at me."

Watson's sister had a somewhat different view of the event. She claims that Watson was taken off the show, not because he was not smart enough, but because he lacked the flashy personality for which the show's producers were looking.

Watson's early interest in science was only lukewarm. As a boy, he often accompanied his father on bird-watching trips around Chicago. Later, at the University of Chicago, ornithology (the study of birds) seemed to be the only field of science in which he was really interested. He told friends that his ambition was to become curator of birds at New York City's American Museum of Natural History. And, in the summer of 1946, Watson took a course in advanced ornithology at the University of Michigan. Still, in looking back on those days, Watson claims that ornithology had been only "a way of playing at science."

One of the striking parallels between the lives of Watson and Crick is the role of one or two influential books in molding their thinking and later careers. The first of these books in Watson's life was Sinclair Lewis's novel *Arrowsmith. Arrowsmith* is the story of an American doctor and his intense commitment to science. Watson says that the novel started him thinking about the possibility of making "great discoveries" in science. He realized that he was interested in becoming not a "dried up academic," but someone who was "famous in science."

But where was the problem through which he could gain that fame? The answer to that question came in the second book that influenced Watson's life, Schrodinger's *What Is Life?* Watson realized that the key connection between atoms and molecules on the one hand, and the nature of life on the other hand, was the gene. The scientist who could unravel the chemical and physical code by which genes carried hereditary messages was assured of the fame for which Watson hoped.

The coincidence is remarkable. Separated by more than a decade in age and living continents apart, Crick and Watson were set on similar paths by the same book.

Watson applied to do graduate study first at Harvard and then at the California Institute of Technology. His applications were rejected by both institutions. Looking back, these rejections were probably blessings in disguise because Watson then turned to his third choice, Indiana University.

In his application to Indiana, Watson expressed an interest in doing graduate work in ornithology. But that possibility turned out to be quite unlikely. In the first place, Indiana had no program in ornithology. The dean of the graduate school wrote Watson that if he really wanted to study birds, he "should go somewhere else." In the second place, Indiana did have Hermann J. Muller. Muller was one of the greatest geneticists alive. He had won the Nobel Prize in 1946 for his research on the genetic effects of X rays. With Watson's newly awakened interest in the gene, Indiana seemed very much like the institution where he could do his doctoral research. He was accepted, given a research fellowship of $900 and enrolled in the fall of 1947.

Once enrolled at Indiana, Watson's logical choice for a doctoral advisor was Muller. But Watson had become convinced that fruit flies—Muller's special area of interest—were too "biological" for his tastes. They did not seem to be a promising subject of study for his new interest in the physical nature of the gene.

Instead, he turned his attention to another hot topic of interest among some researchers: phages. The word *phage* is shorthand for the term *bacteriophage*. Bacteriophages are a type of virus that attack, infect, and destroy bacteria. By the early 1940s, some scientists had begun to believe that studies of phages would provide the best possible information on the nature of genes and of heredity. Watson has said that at the time he entered Indiana, "the suspicion had existed among the more inspired geneticists that viruses were a form of naked genes."

Viruses, including phages, lie on the borderline between the living and nonliving. They consist of a few very large molecules that perform many—but not all—of the functions of living organisms.

The most important of these molecules are nucleic acids. Nucleic acids are the chemical compounds that carry the genetic information stored in an organism. The nucleic acids in a phage are encased within a "coat," or *capsid*. The capsid is formed primarily of protein and protects the phage's nucleic acid from attack by enzymes and other substances that would otherwise destroy it.

Phages, like other viruses, can not reproduce by themselves. They remain dormant and lifeless until and unless they infect another cell. Figure 1 shows what happens after infection occurs.

Two of the leading researchers on bacteriophages in the 1940s were on the Indiana faculty, Salvatore Luria and Max Delbruck. Luria was an Italian who had trained in medicine and immigrated to the United States in 1940. Delbruck was a German who had trained as a physicist and immigrated to the U.S. in 1937.

Delbruck's name was already well known to Watson. It was his ideas about the physical nature of the gene that had been described in Schrodinger's *What Is Life?*

Delbruck's own ideas on this subject had, in turn, been influenced by Niels Bohr, the great Danish physicist. In an address in 1932, Bohr had presented the reductionist argument for studying the molecules of living organisms. "If we were able to push the analysis of the mechanism of living organisms as far as that of atomic phenomena," Bohr had said, "we should scarcely expect to find any features differing from the properties of inorganic matter."

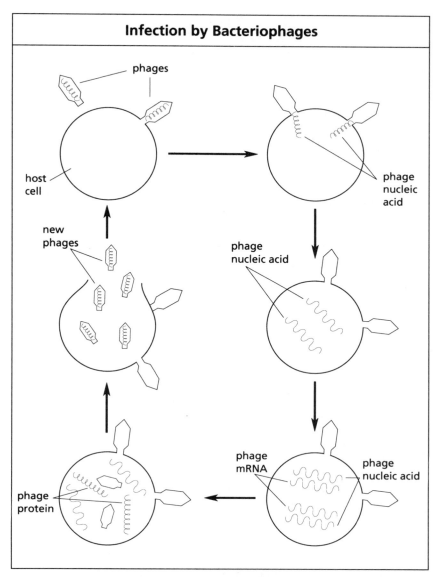

Infection by Bacteriophages

Figure 1: First, a phage attaches itself to the surface of the host cell. Then, nucleic acid from the phage is injected into the host cell. The presence of phage nucleic acid causes the host cell's own reproductive system to shut down. Instead, the host cell begins to "read" and carry out instructions stored in the phage nucleic acid. The host cell makes new copies of phage nucleic acid and of phage protein. Finally, new phage particles are assembled and then released from the host cell. The host cell may be destroyed in the process.

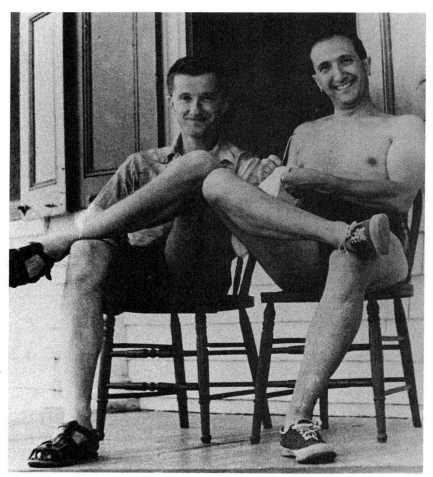

Max Delbruck (left) and Salvatore Luria at Cold Spring Harbor in 1941.
(Cold Spring Harbor Laboratory)

Along with a handful of other scientists around the country, Luria and Delbruck thought of themselves as "the American phage group." The American phage group included, in addition to Luria and Delbruck, the most important scientists working on phage research. It was into this group that James Watson moved soon after his arrival at Indiana. And it was Luria whom Watson asked to serve as his doctoral advisor.

During his thee years at Indiana, Watson worked on a special phage problem to which Luria had assigned him. It was a line of research that eventually proved not to be very productive. But it did allow Watson to receive his doctorate in May of 1950, at the age of 22.

Watson's thesis research often took a back seat to the activities of the phage group. These activities usually seemed more interesting and proved to be ultimately more valuable than his own doctoral research. Among these activities was his first visit in 1948 to the Cold Spring Harbor biological laboratory on Long Island. The Cold Spring Harbor Laboratory of Quantitative Biology is a nonprofit organization famous for the courses, meetings, and research opportunities it provides for biologists from all over the world.

Among the major events that occur at Cold Spring Harbor (CSH) is the annual Symposium on Quantitative Biology. Each year, the greatest biologists in the world attend the symposium. During the late 1940s and early 1950s, members of the phage group met informally during the symposium, exchanging ideas and reports of their research. The sessions were lively and invigorating, perhaps as exciting as any scientific meeting in the United States. Watson reports of his first summer at CSH that

The Cold Spring Harbor Laboratory of Quantitative Biology. (Cold Spring Harbor Laboratory)

As the summer passed on I liked Cold Spring Harbor more and more, both for its intrinsic beauty and for the honest ways in which good and bad science got sorted out.

Much of the success of the phage group meetings has been attributed to Delbruck. One writer has credited him with

creating at Cold Spring Harbor that spirit of ceaseless questioning, dialogue, and open-armed embrace of a life in science which he had learned from Bohr*—but with a down-to-earth American character and a good measure of his open high-minded intolerance of shoddy thinking.

The Cold Spring Harbor experience reminds one that students learn a great deal more than facts from their teachers. They learn ways of attacking problems, attitudes about their subject matter, philosophies of life, and methods for dealing with the world. Thus, Watson left Indiana with a great deal more than a doctoral degree in biology.

He has said, for example, that Delbruck and Luria made science seem "like fun and games." Delbruck in particular taught him not to be too neat and precise in his experiments but to make use of "inspired sloppiness." Experiments that are too carefully designed, Delbruck warned, might prevent one from seeing unexpected, but important, results.

Watson has also credited Luria and Delbruck with helping him to gain confidence. His teachers encouraged him not to fear being different and to speak his mind as to what he believed. Then, they backed him up and provided support when he needed it.

As Watson's work at Indiana came to an end, he began to think about his next move. Frequently a person who has finished a doctoral degree will go on to further study and research in a post-doctoral program. Luria, Delbruck, and Watson's discussions about his post-doctoral plans focused on a new aspect of the gene problem: recent discoveries concerning nucleic acids.

As mentioned earlier, biologists had long thought that proteins were likely candidates to be the molecules that carry genetic information. But there was some reason to believe that a second

---

*Niels Bohr, Danish physicist and winner of the Nobel Prize in 1922 for his model of the atom.

family of chemical compounds, the nucleic acids, might have that role.

Nucleic acids were first discovered in 1868 by the Swiss chemist Johan Freidrich Miescher. Miescher originally named these compounds *nuclein* because he found them in the nuclei, or central area, of cells. They were later given their modern name of nucleic acids. The term *nucleic acid* applies to a great variety of compounds, some of which occur in other parts of the cell than the nucleus. Nucleic acids exist in one of two forms, deoxyribonucleic acid (DNA) and ribonucleic acid (RNA).

Almost as soon as Miescher discovered nucleic acid, the possibility was presented that this new category of compounds might be the genetic material. The German zoologist, Oskar Hertwig, wrote in 1884 that "nuclein is the substance that is responsible not only for fertilisation but also for the transmission of hereditary characteristics."

The problem was that nucleic acids did not seem to be complex enough to carry genetic information. They certainly appeared to be far less complex than proteins. The proteins found in humans, for example, are made of various combinations of 20 different amino acids. The number of different protein molecules that can be made from all possible combinations of these 20 different amino acids is staggeringly large (see page 9).

But nucleic acids seemed to be much simpler compounds. Their molecules consist of only a simple sugar, a phosphate group (a phosphorus atom with four oxygens attached to it), and five relatively simple nitrogen compounds, or nitrogen bases.

The most widely accepted model of the nucleic acids was that developed by the Russian biochemist Phoebus Levene in the early 1900s. Levene suggested that nucleic acids consisted of long chains of sugar and phosphate groups, with one nitrogen base attached to each sugar group. He thought the bases were probably arranged in some simple, orderly fashion, such as base 1 – base 2 – base 3 – base 4 – base 1 – base 2 – base 3 – base 4 – and so on. This model eventually was called the *tetranucleotide hypothesis* of nucleic acid structure.

If that model were correct, then the nucleic acids were boring, uninteresting molecules. There certainly didn't seem to be any way that they could carry very much genetic information since they could not exist in many different forms. Scientists generally regarded the nucleic acids as being "dumb" molecules because they did not appear capable of carrying much genetic information.

Still, experimental evidence contradicting this view had existed for a long time. According to one historian of science, John Gribbin, research on salmon sperm conducted in the 1890s was actually conclusive enough to show that the hereditary information in at least this organism *must* be carried by DNA.

Probably the most important experiments on the role of DNA in heredity had been reported in 1944 by three American physicians, Oswald T. Avery, Colin M. MacLeod, and Maclyn McCarthy. The Avery team had been able to show that the kind of bacteria that grow in an experiment depended on the kind of DNA the bacteria contained. They could change one kind of bacteria into a different kind by removing the bacteria's original DNA and replacing it with a second kind of DNA. The Avery experiments were thoroughly and carefully done. Evidence for the controlling role of DNA in determining heredity seemed very strong.

In looking back, the Avery experiments seem very convincing. They seem to show clearly how important nucleic acids are in heredity. Yet, scientists often cling to familiar ideas long after they are no longer valid. Avery's experiments were not fully understood or accepted, especially outside of the United States, for a half-dozen years after the work had been completed. In 1950, the great majority of biologists still thought that genes were made entirely, or to a large extent, of proteins, not nucleic acids.

There were at least two important exceptions to this statement: Francis Crick and James Watson. Both had come to believe that DNA was the key hereditary material. They were convinced that unraveling the nature of the gene was going to require a much better understanding of the chemical and physical structure of DNA. But that presented a problem for Watson. He claims that he knew very little chemistry. He had never liked chemistry very well and had avoided it wherever possible. At Indiana, he claims that he had posed such a danger in the chemistry laboratory that he had been "relieved from further true chemistry." After having been found heating a highly flammable liquid, Watson reports, his professors decided that it was "safer to turn out an uneducated Ph.D. than to risk another explosion."*

Yet it was now clear that an understanding of biochemistry, or the chemistry of living things, was critical if Watson was to continue his quest for the structure of the gene. As a result, Luria recommended that Watson spend his first postdoctoral year with Herman Kalckar, a Danish biochemist at the University of Copenhagen. Kalckar had attended one of Delbruck's courses on phages at Cold Spring Harbor in 1945. He was currently working on phages and nucleic acids in Copenhagen.

Luria helped Watson obtain a fellowship from the National Research Council for 1950–51. The fellowship paid $3,000 a year and was renewable after the first year. In the fall of 1950, Watson left for Denmark.

Watson's year at Copenhagen was a great disappointment, as he has written, "a complete flop." He hated the weather, found the work uninteresting and irrelevant, and missed the intellectual companionship that he had experienced at Indiana and in the phage group. Kalckar was preoccupied with personal problems of his own and provided little inspiration for Watson.

As the year grew to a close, Watson realized that he had to make a change. Two events helped him decide on his next course of action. The first was a chance meeting with Maurice Wilkins at a scientific meeting in Naples. Wilkens was an X-ray crystallographer, then with Professor J. T. Randall at King's College in London.

Wilkins's lecture at the Naples meeting included some X-ray photographs of a DNA molecule. Watson was fascinated by what he saw. Here was concrete physical evidence that could be used in understanding the gene. If genes could be crystallized, like most ordinary chemicals, then they could be studied by ordinary chemical and physical methods. As Watson said, "Suddenly I was excited about chemistry."

---

*Robert Olby, who has written a history of the search for DNA, has disputed this point. He reminds us that Watson successfully completed a number of chemistry courses at both Chicago and Indiana.

A Helix

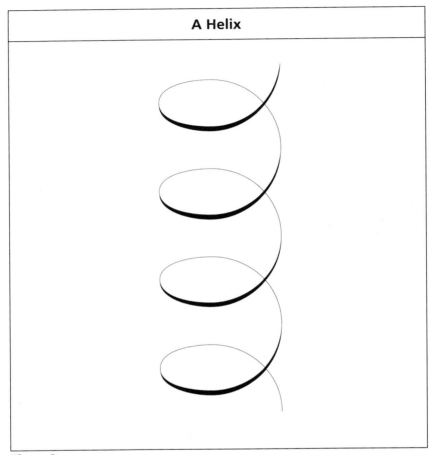

Figure 2

Watson wanted to find out more about Wilkins's work. He decided to introduce his sister, Elizabeth, to Wilkins, hoping that they would become attracted to each other. With his sister as a go-between, Watson hoped to become a close friend of Wilkins and learn more about the kind of work the English physicist was doing. His efforts at playing matchmaker were not successful, however, and Wilkins left Naples without having spent any time with Watson.

The second event occurred a few days later. Watson heard that Linus Pauling, at the California Institute of Technology, had worked out the three-dimensional structure of proteins. According to Pauling's model, the atoms in a protein are arranged in a helix. A helix is a spiral structure that looks something like a Slinky toy that has been stretched too much. The atoms in the molecule are arranged in a coil, as shown in Figure 2.

Linus Pauling is one of the giants of modern chemistry. Watson had held Pauling in the highest esteem since his days at Indiana. Now, within a few days of seeing Wilkins's X-ray photos of DNA, Watson read of Pauling's remarkable discoveries about the structure of proteins.

Watson was now convinced that he had to learn more about X-ray crystallography. Having heard of Max Perutz's work at Cambridge, Watson wrote Luria about having his fellowship transferred to the Cavendish Laboratory at Cambridge. Convinced that he would have no problem in making this change, Watson left Copenhagen in the fall of 1951. He arrived in Cambridge and went directly from the train station to Perutz's office. The most momentous two years of his life were about to begin.

CHAPTER 2 NOTES

p. 11   "real expectations . . ." Robert Olby, "Francis Crick, DNA, and the Central Dogma," *Daedalus* (Fall 1970): p. 938.

p. 11   "must have been very keen . . ." "James Dewey Watson," *Current Biography Yearbook, 1963* (New York: H.W. Wilson, 1963), p. 59.

p. 11   "he never took any notes . . ." Lois N. Magner, *A History of the Life Sciences* (New York: Marcel Dekker, 1979), p. 456.

p. 11   "it was an awful job . . ." Stephen S. Hall, "James Watson and the search for biology's 'Holy Grail,'" *Smithsonian* (February 1990): p. 42.

p. 12   "between the steel mills . . ." Will Bradbury, "Genius on the prowl," Life (October 30, 1970): p. 59.

p. 12   "If I had known . . ." Hall, "James Watson," p. 43.

p. 12   "a way of playing . . ." Horace Freeland Judson, *The Eighth Day of Creation* (New York: Simon and Schuster, 1979), p. 47.

p. 13   "great discoveries," etc. Lee Edson, "Says Nobelist James (Double Helix) Watson, 'To Hell with Being Discovered when You're Dead'" *New York Times Magazine* (August 18, 1968): p. 34

p. 13   "should go somewhere else," Judson, *The Eighth Day,* p. 47

p. 14   "the suspicion . . ." James D. Watson, *The Double Helix* (New York: Atheneum, 1968), p. 22.

p. 14   "if we were able . . ." As quoted in John Gribbin, *In Search of the Double Helix,* p. 214.

p. 18   "As the summer . . ." Judson, *The Eighth Day,* p. 67.

p. 18   "like fun and games," etc. Edson, "Says Nobelist," p. 34.

p. 19   "nuclein is the substance . . ." As quoted in Alfred Mirsky, "The Discovry of DNA," *Scientific American* (June 1968): p. 78.

p. 21   "safer to turn out . . ." Watson, *Double Helix,* p. 22.

3

THE SEARCH BEGINS

A drama was about to unfold at the Cavendish Laboratory. No playwright could ask for a better cast and a more intriguing story. The two main actors were Francis Crick and James Watson. They were both, themselves, enormously interesting men. But even more interesting was the way in which they complemented each other and worked together.

Crick was a 35-year-old Englishman, just beginning his doctoral studies. Watson was 12 years younger, with a Ph.D. earned at the age of 22. Contemporaries and biographers have described Crick with phrases such as "a brash, brilliant eccentric given to manic bursts of energy, peals of raucous laughter, loud and rapid speech, and an honesty of expression that some find abrasive and others tactless" or "famous for his wild but brilliant conceptual leaps"; Watson as a "brash, bitter-tongued biologist" who at the age of 23 was "impatient, a bit lazy, always dreaming of women and fame."

Both were also on the fringes of their own scientific disciplines. Crick had come to a study of the DNA molecule from physics, Watson from genetics. Neither had any previous background in the research to which they were now committed: the chemical and physical analysis of crystals. Both were self-taught, or learned much of what they needed to know on the job. Although their backgrounds made their task more difficult in some ways, it also allowed them to look at their problem in fresh, new ways.

More important than any differences in personality and professional background were the ideas the two men shared. Both were convinced that the structure of DNA was a fundamental question—perhaps the fundamental question—in biology. They suspected that a few other scientists were close to solving the problem of DNA's structure. And they were both committed to the same technique for unraveling the puzzle of DNA: building physical models of the molecule.

Neither Watson nor Crick remembers the exact circumstances of their first meeting in October of 1951. But both recall that something special occurred at that meeting. Almost immediately, each realized that the other was thinking about DNA, genes, and heredity as almost no one else in the world was. Crick has said that he was "electrified" on meeting Watson. "It was remarkable," he said, "because we both had the same point of view."

On Watson's part, he regarded it as "real luck" that he had found someone at the Cavendish who "knew that DNA was more important than protein." He remembers that "From the first day in the lab I knew I would not leave Cambridge for a long time. Departing would be idiocy, for I had immediately discovered the fun of talking to Francis Crick."

The match between these two seemingly diverse geniuses was so perfect that, as one writer has said, "They evidently fell into a kind of intellectual crush on each other."

Another observer has also described the relationship between Crick and Watson as a kind of intellectual "love."

> There has to be an extraordinary interaction between two people, before the mind can do what they did. Jim and Francis talked in half sentences. They understood each other almost without words . . . That marvelous resonance between two minds—that high state in which one plus one does not equal two but more like ten.

Thus began, in the late fall of 1951, one of the great dialogues in the history of science. Crick and Watson were soon having lunch together nearly every day at a local pub, the Eagle. Eventually they were even assigned to their own office together, away from other researchers. The reason seemed to be so that the two could "talk to each other and not disturb the rest of [the scientists]."

The point of these conversations quickly centered on the task Watson and Crick saw for themselves. They had to figure out exactly how the DNA molecule was put together. In this task, it seemed possible that they were in a race with a man whom many

Watson and Crick in their office at the Cavendish Laboratory. (Cold Spring Harbor Laboratory)

considered to be the world's greatest biochemist, Linus Pauling. They decided that the best way to beat Pauling in the race was to use his own method of model building.

In the 1950s, model building was a technique almost unknown among biologists. However, Pauling had demonstrated what a powerful tool it could be in analyzing the structure of complex molecules. Tinker-toy-like models allowed a scientist to see exactly how atoms fit together in molecules. The "tinker-toy" atoms could be moved around in all sorts of ways until the molecules they built fit the experimental data known about the molecules.

X-ray photographs of crystals were a key part of model building. From these photographs, a scientist can calculate the distances between atoms, the angles at which they are attached to each other, the ways atoms are grouped together, and so on.

X-ray photographs of large molecules always presented two problems, however. First, it was often difficult to get really good photographs of a molecule. This was especially true of the large, complex molecules found in living organisms, such as protein and nucleic acid molecules. Second, any one X-ray photograph could often be interpreted in more than one way. The problem was to figure out which tinker-toy model was the correct structure for any one X-ray photograph.

Watson and Crick had a fair amount of data with which to begin their model building. First, they knew that DNA consists of three smaller groups: a sugar molecule, a phosphate group, and four types of nitrogen-containing molecules called bases. The structures of these three groups are shown in Figure 3.

Second, chemists had already learned how these three groups were joined together in a DNA molecule. The combination of a sugar, a phosphate, and one nitrogen base was called a nucleotide. The structure of one nucleotide is shown in Figure 4 on page 30.

Third, the DNA molecule was known to consist of a long chain of nucleotides, as shown in Figure 5 on page 31. The chain contains alternate sugar and phosphate groups, with one nitrogen base extending off each sugar. The chain is also called a *polynucleotide* because it contains many ("poly") nucleotides joined to each other.

Finally, the DNA molecule was thought to exist in the form of a spiral, called a helix. Figure 2, on page 22 shows what a helix looks like. The DNA helix was thought to be made of the sugar-phosphate chain, with the nitrogen bases sticking off the chain.

It may seem that a great deal was already known about the DNA molecule. What was left to discover? The puzzle that Crick and Watson needed to solve involved all the details of this picture. For example, did the DNA molecule consist of only one helix, or did it contain two, three, or even four helices? Did the nitrogen bases stick outward from the helix, or were they buried somewhere inside it? How tightly was the DNA helix wound? How much space was there between coils in the helix. And so on. (Many of the problems to be solved for the DNA molecule are too complicated to describe in this book.)

The decision by Watson and Crick to study DNA structure created some awkward problems. That line of research was already going on at King's College in London. Getting official permission from their superiors to do similar research at Cavendish would

The Components of DNA Molecule

sugar molecule

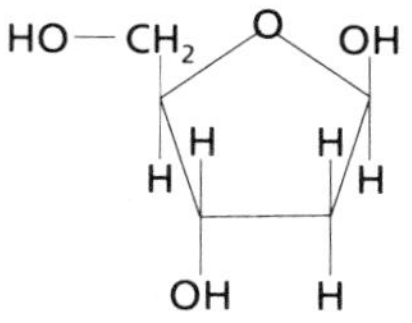

phosphate group

2-deoxyribose

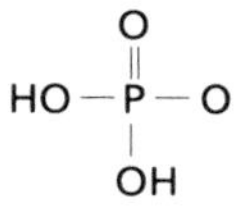

four nitrogen bases

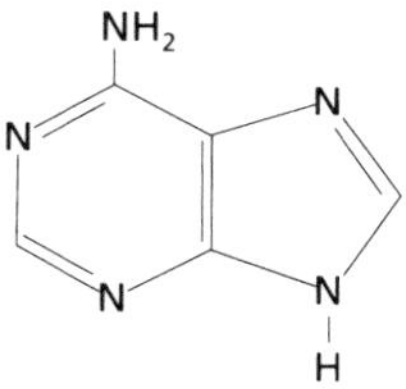

adenine 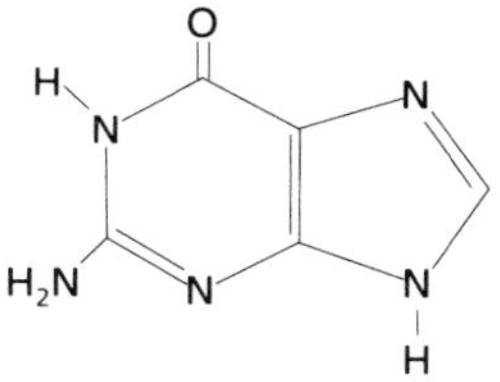   guanine 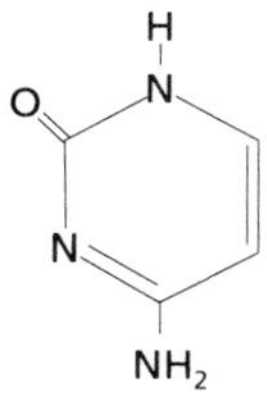   cytosine 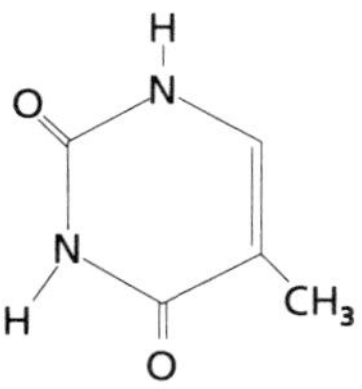   thymine

key:

O = oxygen atom
H = hydrogen atom
N = nitrogen atom
P = phosphorus atom

A carbon atom is understood to be located at the intersection of any four lines in a formula.

A single line (———) in a formula represents a single covalent bond, that is, a pair of shared electrons.

A double line (═══) in a formula represents a double covalent bond, that is, two pairs of shared electrons.

Figure 3

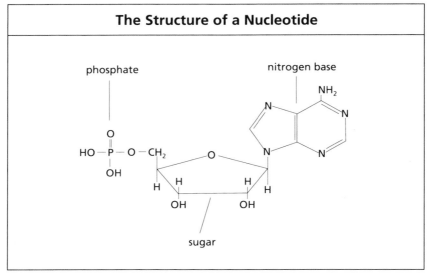

The Structure of a Nucleotide

Figure 4

have created a difficult professional dilemma for Watson and Crick. Researchers at King's already had established priority in this line of research, and it would have been improper for anyone at Cavendish to "horn in" on the topic. The problem was especially acute for Crick because the King's research was going on under the direction of his good friend, Maurice Wilkins.

In a more practical vein, research funds were tight. It would have been difficult to ask the government to fund what would look like duplicate research on DNA at two institutions, King's and Cavendish.

Besides, both Crick and Watson already had assignments at the Cavendish, Crick his doctoral research and Watson his work on viruses under the direction of John Kendrew.

In fact, Crick and Watson did not allow any of these considerations to interfere with their interest in DNA. They decided to go ahead and see what they could learn about the structure of this fascinating molecule.

They constructed their first model of DNA in less than a week. Of course, an enormous amount of talking and thinking had

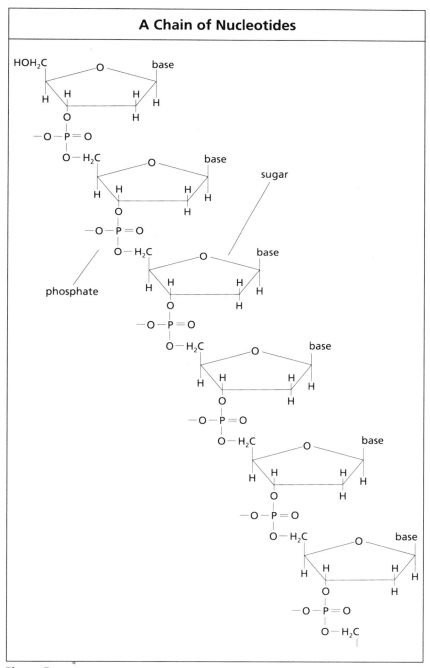

A Chain of Nucleotides

Figure 5

preceded this spurt of model building. But the time between initial concept and final model for this first effort was remarkably brief.

The key event leading to this trial was a lecture given by Rosalind Franklin, a crystallographer working in Wilkins's laboratory. Watson attended a lecture of hers, given on November 21, 1951, at King's College, London.

The main points of Franklin's lecture are preserved in her handwritten notes for the lecture and in a formal report she wrote three months later. She thought that fibers of DNA might have a cylindrical structure, like that shown in Figure 6. The cylinder she proposed was made of nucleic acid chains coiled around the axis of the cylinder. Franklin was uncertain whether there were two, three, or four chains in the cylinder.

She further supposed that the sugar-phosphate backbone of the chains was on the outside of the cylinder and the nitrogen bases inside. She suggested that adjacent DNA fibers might be held together by metallic bonds between them. In Figure 6 these metallic bonds are represented by sodium ions (Na^+) joined to each cylinder by dotted lines. (Ions are atoms or groups of atoms with either a positive or a negative electrical charge.)

Franklin made it clear that her results were only preliminary. Until she was able to prepare better DNA samples and make clearer photographs, her initial model was still very speculative, she said. But this was Franklin's style. She was always very cautious and conservative in announcing the results of her research, preferring to wait until she had stronger evidence before making more positive statements about possible shapes of molecules.

As was his custom, Watson took no notes on the lecture, trusting to his usually reliable memory the main points of Franklin's talk. The problem was that this time Watson's memory failed him. He later explained that he knew too little crystallography to understand everything Franklin said. Moreover, some of what he thought he recalled, he remembered incorrectly. His most important error concerned the amount of water attached to DNA molecules. Franklin estimated that each nucleotide in a DNA molecule was surrounded by about eight water molecules. Watson misunderstood and thought that she said there were about eight water

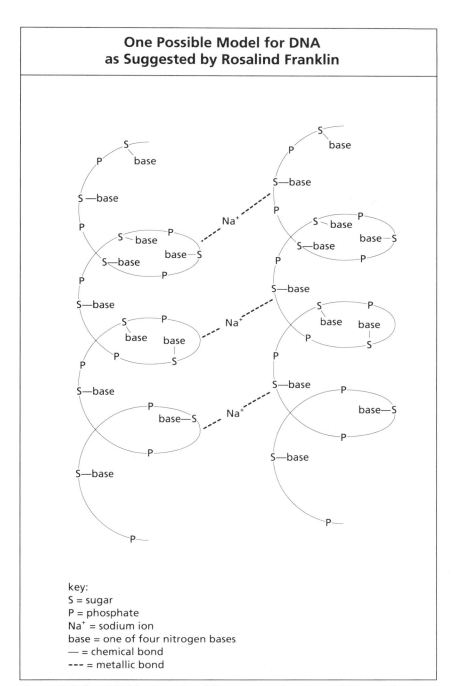

Figure 6: In her 1951 lecture, Franklin suggested one possible model for the DNA molecule.

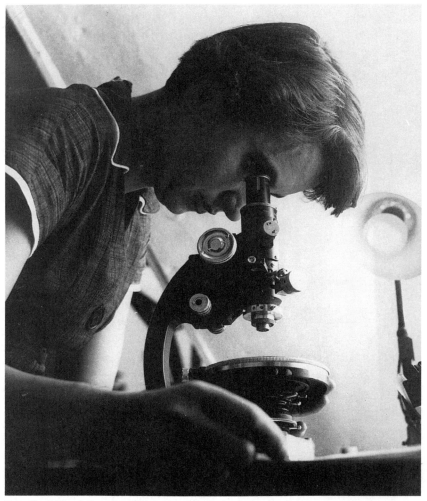

Rosalind Franklin. (Medical Research Council Laboratory of Molecular Biology, photo by Henry Grant AIIP, courtesy of Mrs. Jennifer Glynn)

molecules in each segment of the molecule. The figure that Watson remembered was therefore far too small.

The consequence of Watson's mistake was to become apparent all too soon. On the very next morning, Watson and Crick traveled from London to Oxford together. During the trip, Watson reported to Crick his recollection of the Franklin lecture, including the erroneous data.

Crick was annoyed that Watson had failed to take notes at the lecture. He realized that Watson's report might contain some incorrect or misleading data. Still, he was eager to try sketching some models of DNA that would fit the data Watson had given him.

Before long he informed Watson that the number of possible models was really quite small. Two of the most important decisions that had to be made about the possible models were the number of polynucleotide chains in the DNA molecule and the position of the nitrogen bases on the sugar-phosphate chains (inside or outside of the molecule).

But Crick was optimistic that these problems could be solved relatively easily. Watson recalls that

> By the time the hour-and-a-half train journey was over, Francis saw no reason why we should not know the answer soon. Perhaps a week of fiddling with the molecular models would be necessary to make us absolutely sure we had the right answer. Then it would be obvious to the world that Pauling was not the only one capable of true insight into how biological molecules were constructed.

Four days later, Crick and Watson were in the laboratory, constructing models of Francis's idea. They worked with jigs (model pieces) that had been designed for proteins and were the wrong size and shape for nucleic acids. Atoms kept falling off the model, and progress was slow at first.

The first model they worked with involved two polynucleotide chains wrapped around each other in a helix. But they could not make the model fit the (incorrect) data that Watson had remembered from Franklin's lecture.

A three-chain model seemed to work better. Watson and Crick were a little uncomfortable with this version, however, because some atoms did not seem to fit together properly. But then, as Watson observed, "the fiddling had just begun." If they only stayed with the work a little longer, they thought, they might be able to come up with a reasonable product.

Only 24 hours after they had begun, Watson and Crick had a model that they felt confident about. It was a three-chain model with the sugar-phosphate backbone on the inside and the nitrogen bases on the outside. Most important, the model corresponded with the crystallographic data that Watson thought Franklin had reported. A day later, they invited Wilkins, Franklin, and other colleagues to examine their final product.

To their chagrin, Franklin immediately found an error in the model. The error had resulted from Watson's incorrect reporting of her data. She pointed out that the Watson-Crick molecule would hold only a fraction of the water that it actually held, a piece of information she had reported in her November lecture.

The model, she insisted, was totally inconsistent with the information she had obtained in her research. In fact, according to Watson's account, Franklin felt that "there was not a shred of evidence that DNA was helical."

Watson's statement is probably somewhat incorrect. In both her November 1951 lecture on DNA and her February 1952 notes on the subject, Franklin admitted that DNA might exist as a helix. Her point, however, was that it was still too soon to start making models of the molecule. Much more research had to be done first.

This viewpoint illustrates how differently Wilkins and Franklin on the one hand and Watson and Crick on the other approached the problem of DNA structure. For the former, the primary goal was to collect as much information about the character of DNA as possible. When those data were in, then scientists could begin speculating on the molecular structure.

Watson and Crick started at the opposite end of the problem. They began building models as soon as they could. Then they tested those models against the existing data, however incomplete they might be. Both Watson and Crick were always concerned about being mislead by incorrect or incomplete data.

In any case, Watson and Crick had failed in this, their first model-building attempt. They had been badly thrown off by Watson's incorrect remembrance of Franklin's vital data about the water content of DNA. As a result, they had gone from high hopes to an apparently promising model to defeat in less than a week.

The November 1951 fiasco had a cooling effect on Crick and Watson's efforts to solve the DNA problem. Bragg was unhappy about the event, and he sent down word that the two men were to abandon this line of research. He pointed out that Wilkins, Franklin, and the King's College team had been working on DNA structure well before Watson and Crick. Professional courtesy demanded that King's, not Cavendish, be given priority on this line of research. Bragg told Watson and Crick to turn over the jigs for their DNA model to Wilkins. (As it turned out, Wilkins did not want or use the jigs. His approach, like that of Franklin, was to concentrate on collecting data through experimentation, rather than model building.)

Bragg also told Watson and Crick to return to their "real" work at the Cavendish. After all, neither was really supposed to be working on DNA at all. Crick had a doctoral dissertation to complete. His topic concerned the X-ray diffraction of polypeptides and proteins. Crick never seemed particularly interested in the topic. It was just something he had to do to earn his degree. Indeed, instead of working on his thesis, Crick had spent much of his time since arriving at the Cavendish moving "from problem to problem, doing other men's crosswords but not finishing his own."

Meanwhile, Watson had his own assignments too. According to the terms of his fellowship, he was supposed to be working on plant viruses with Professor Roy Markham. He had also been assigned to assist John Kendrew in the growing of protein crystals.

With the failure of their first DNA model, both Watson and Crick reluctantly returned to their official assignments at the Cavendish.

But neither man could get DNA out of his mind. Both knew that they could not go back to model building in their laboratory. But that did not prevent them from reading, talking, and thinking about the DNA puzzle. And so, in spite of Bragg's instructions, DNA remained the secret obsession of both men.

At the same time, both Crick and Watson had personal lives of their own, of course. That statement may seem trite. But it is sometimes easy to think of scientists as men and women in white coats who spend all their time with beakers and microscopes.

One can learn something of the Crick household from passages in Watson's later book, *The Double Helix*. Watson describes the Crick home, Green Door, as a "tiny, inexpensive flat on top of a several-hundred-year-old house." Although the flat was cramped, Crick's wife Odile had made it into a "cheerful, if not playful," living space. It was in this home, Watson writes, that he first sensed "the vitality of English intellectual life."

Odile was Crick's second wife. His first marriage in 1940 to Doreen Dodd lasted until 1947. The only child of that marriage, Michael, was born on November 25, 1940, during an air raid. Crick married the former Odile Speed in 1949. Two daughters, Gabrielle and Jacqueline, were born to Odile and Francis.

Watson especially appreciated his time at Green Door because of its contrast with his own lodgings in Cambridge. He remained for only a month in the first room he rented after arriving in Cambridge. He reports that his major "crimes" were "not removing my shoes when I entered the house after 9:00 P.M.," forgetting not to flush the toilet at late hours, and going out after 10:00 P.M. Since nothing in Cambridge was open that late, he points out, his "motives were suspect." As a result, his landlady "kicked him

John C. Kendrew with a model of the myoglobin molecule, whose structure he determined. (Medical Research Council Laboratory of Molecular Biology)

Watson, on vacation in the Italian Alps, August 1952. (Cold Spring Harbor Laboratory, Research Library Archives)

out," and he took a room with the Kendrews. John Kendrew was a member of Perutz's research team. The room that he and his wife offered Watson turned out to be "unbelievably damp" and "an open invitation to tuberculosis." Nonetheless, he was delighted with the new housing arrangements.

Another factor contributing to Watson's modest lodgings was the surprising news that his fellowship from the National Research Council (NRC) had not been renewed. His request to transfer to the Perutz group at Cambridge had been rejected. There was nothing in Watson's background, the new director at NRC decided, that qualified him to do research in X-ray crystallography.

Of course, that fact was true. Thus, the decision to cancel Watson's fellowship must have made complete sense to a disinterested observer in the fall of 1951, but the fact was that Watson was already in Cambridge, deeply involved in research related to X-ray crystallography. Furthermore, he had no intention of leaving Cambridge for Copenhagen or for the NRC's recommended alternative to Copenhagen, Torbjorn Caspersson's biochemistry lab in Stockholm.

The matter was eventually resolved by resorting to a certain amount of subterfuge. The NRC was told that Watson would begin work at a Cambridge biology laboratory, the Molteno Institute, under the laboratory's director, Dr. Roy Markham. Watson would be doing research on viruses that attack plants, the NRC was assured.

The council accepted this arrangement. It extended Watson's fellowship to May of 1952 at a reduced rate of $2,000. The fact that Watson never had any intention of working with Markham was clear to everyone involved . . . except the NRC. Watson's financial needs for the next seven months, however, were now provided for. He could return to the pursuit that had become the driving force of his life and of Francis Crick's—unraveling the structure of DNA.

CHAPTER 3 NOTES

p. 25   "a brash, brilliant . . ." Pamela Weintraub, "Sperm from deep space: Francis Crick," *The Omni Interviews* (New York: Ticknor & Fields, 1984), p. 22.

p. 25   "famous for his . . ." Daniel Goleman, "Crick's twitch," *Psychology Today* (August, 1982): p. 80.

p. 25   "brash, bitter-tongued . . ." Will Bradbury, "Genius on the Prowl," *Life* (October 30, 1970): p. 57.

p. 25   "impatient, a bit lazy . . ." George Johnson, "Two sides to every science story," *New York Times Book Review* (April 9, 1989): p. 39.

p. 26   "It was remarkable . . ." Horace Freeland Judson, *The Eighth Day of Creation* (New York: Simon and Schuster, 1979), p. 112.

p. 26   "From the first day . . ." James D. Watson, *The Double Helix* (New York: Atheneum, 1968), p. 48.

p. 26   "They evidently fell . . ." Judson, *The Eighth Day*, p. 112.

p. 26   "There has to be . . ." As quoted in Judson, *The Eighth Day*, p. 193–94.

p. 26   "Talk to each other . . ." Judson, *The Eighth Day*, pp. 111–112.

p. 35   "By the time . . ." Watson, *Double Helix*, p. 77.

p. 36   "there was not a shred . . ." Watson, *Double Helix*, p. 94.

p. 37   "from problem to problem . . ." Judson, *The Eighth Day*, p. 110.

p. 37   "cheerful, if not playful," etc. Watson, *Double Helix*, pp. 64–65.

p. 38   "crimes," etc. Watson, *Double Helix*, p. 46.

4

TRIALS AND TRIUMPHS

In the early 1960s, James Watson wrote a book describing the search for the structure of the DNA molecule. He called his book *The Double Helix*. The book presents his view of the scientific research and thinking that went into solving the DNA puzzle. But it tells a great deal more than that. It describes the human side of science: the humor, anger, ill-will, ambition, deceit, carelessness, and genius that lay behind this momentous achievement.*

More than a story of atoms and molecules, *The Double Helix* is a tale of people. It explains how a whole cast of characters contributed, immensely and in modest ways, knowingly and unknowingly, eagerly and against their wills, to the discovery of the structure of DNA.

A pivotal figure in this story is Linus Pauling. Pauling has been one of the giants of chemistry for well over half a century. He is one of only three people ever to win two Nobel Prizes, the only person to win two *unshared* prizes. His first Nobel Prize, in 1954, was awarded in chemistry, for his research on chemical bonds and on complex molecules. His second, in 1962, was for peace, awarded because of his efforts to ban the testing of nuclear weapons in the atmosphere.

Pauling's role in the DNA race is, to some extent, that of an innocent bystander. He claims that he and his colleagues did work

---

*The Double Helix has had its share of critics. Many of Watson's colleagues consider the book one-sided and misleading. The controversy over this book will be discussed in more detail in Chapter 7.

on the problem of DNA structure but never viewed their work as a competition. He says that

> We weren't working very hard at it. We had really very little in the way of our own experimental data, a few rather poor X-ray photographs of DNA, not carefully prepared. I wasn't putting in much of my time on determining the structure. I thought I would get it worked out, you know, in a question of time. I didn't know there was competition—that I was involved in any race.

There is little doubt that Pauling had earlier been in a race with Perutz's group at the Cavendish Laboratory on a different problem: the structure of proteins. Pauling won that competition in 1951 when he and Robert Corey published a series of papers on the proteins found in hair, feathers, muscle, tendon, silk, horn, quill,

Linus Pauling. (California Institute of Technology)

gelatin, hemoglobin (the molecule in red blood cells that carries oxygen), and synthetic materials.

These papers, describing a helical structure for protein molecules, were the ones Watson saw upon his return from the Naples conference in April of 1951. Bragg, Perutz, and others at the Cavendish lab were terribly disappointed that they had lost out in this race to Pauling. Bragg especially feared that the Cavendish might suffer a similar embarrassment in the search for the structure of DNA.

Whether or not Pauling saw himself in competition to determine the structure of DNA, Watson certainly viewed things in that light. Horace Freeland Judson, author of *The Eighth Day of Creation*, a book that describes the Watson-Crick discovery, claims that "it was . . . the thought of Pauling he [Watson] employed to whip himself out of neurasthenic lethargies [deep depression] into frenzies of work." On the other hand, Crick has insisted on a number of occasions that he never viewed the search for DNA structure as any kind of competition with Pauling.

Regardless of how Watson and Crick felt about the idea of a race with Pauling, the fact remains that they were always very aware of the fact that Pauling might well announce an answer to the DNA puzzle at any moment. At one point, they actually thought they had lost the race to Pauling. The messenger of this news was Pauling's son, Peter.

Peter Pauling had come to Cambridge to work as a research assistant under John Kendrew. He had been assigned office space with Crick and Watson and had become particularly good friends with his slightly older American colleague.

As a result of that friendship, Watson learned in November of 1952 that the elder Pauling had worked out a structure for DNA. For the next two months, Crick and Watson waited in agony for Pauling's official paper, announcing his discovery. Had the great American chemist once more reached an important goal before Cavendish scientists?

The answer came in late January of 1953. Pauling sent a copy of his paper directly to Peter at Cambridge. He proposed a model consisting of three chains, with the sugar-phosphate backbone on the inside and the bases on the outside. Within moments of reading the paper, Watson and Crick were ecstatic. Pauling had made a number of serious errors. The DNA model he proposed could not possibly be correct.

Watson expressed amazement at Pauling's errors. "If a student had made a similar mistake," he later wrote, "he would be thought unfit to benefit from Cal Tech's chemistry department [where Pauling was a professor]."

Watson and Crick breathed more easily as they realized that Pauling had not beaten them in the race to find the DNA structure. But they also knew that their reprieve might be a short one. Pauling's colleagues would soon point out his errors. When that happened, Watson predicted, "Linus would not stop until he captured the structure." They had little time to waste in getting back to the DNA puzzle. The race was still on.

The really big questions about DNA structure were relatively few in number. Were the sugar-phosphate chains on the inside or outside of the DNA molecule? How many helices were there? How were the nitrogen bases arranged on the chain?

One possible solution to the last of these questions is shown in Figure 7. In this model, the nitrogen bases are stacked on top of each other, like a pile of plates on a cupboard shelf. Watson and Crick knew early on that this model was incorrect. What alternative arrangement could they find for the nitrogen bases of their model that would fit the experimental data they had?

The answer to that question came from two directions almost at once. The solution depends on the fact that two of the bases, adenine (A) and guanine (G), belong to a family of chemical compounds known as purines (Figure 8—top). The other two bases, cytosine (C) and thymine (T), are classified as pyrimidines (Figure 8—bottom).

In the spring of 1952, Crick had asked a young mathematician at Cambridge, John Griffith, to calculate the ways in which the four nitrogen bases might be attracted to each other. Griffith found that, because of electrical forces, adenine would be attracted to thymine, and cytosine to guanine.

Shortly thereafter, the significance of these results became apparent to Watson and Crick. They were invited by Kendrew to have lunch with Erwin Chargaff, a biochemist at Columbia University.

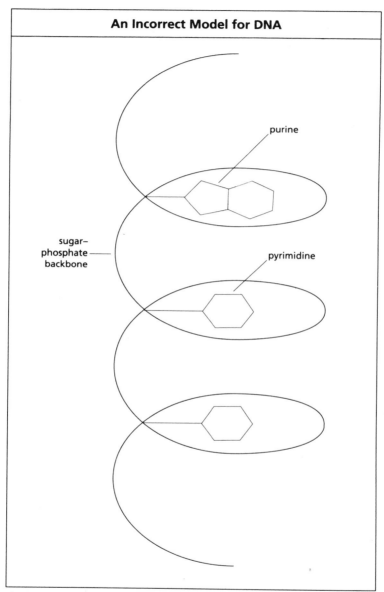

Figure 7: This diagram shows a "stacking" model for DNA, in which the nitrogen bases are "stacked" on top of each other sort of like a pile of plates. From an early point, Watson and Crick knew that this model was wrong.

The Four Nitrogen Bases That Occur in DNA

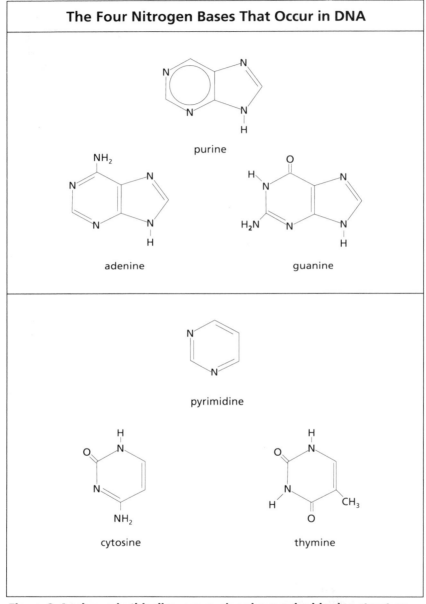

Figure 8: As shown in this diagram, purines have a double-ring structure, whereas pyrimidines have only a single-ring structure.

During luncheon conversation, Crick asked Chargaff what useful information about DNA had been produced by the research in biochemistry so far. Chargaff's answer was "Well, of course, there is the 1:1 ratio."

The "1:1 ratio" to which Chargaff referred had been published three years earlier. The phrase refers to the ratio between nitrogen bases that Chargaff had found in a variety of living materials, including yeast, beef spleen, and calf thymus. Chargaff's research showed that in all of these materials there was an equal amount, or 1:1 ratio, of adenine and thymine and an equal amount of cytosine and guanine.

Crick rather sheepishly admitted that he had never heard of these results. This confession only convinced Chargaff that he was dealing here with two men who were extremely ignorant. He claims that he had "never met two men who knew so little and aspired to so much."

Be that as it may, Crick soon put two and two together. He realized that Griffith's calculations and Chargaff's 1:1 rule both pointed to the same conclusion. The nitrogen bases in DNA must somehow pair with each other: adenine with thymine and cytosine with guanine. Another important piece of the DNA puzzle had fallen into place.

The possibility of base pairing in a DNA molecule had great biological significance. One of the basic questions in genetics had long been how traits are passed from one generation to the next. This process occurs when cells divide. In the early 1950s, scientists knew what happens during "mitosis," or cell division, in terms of structures that can be seen with a microscope.

During *prophase*, the first stage of mitosis, the structures known as *chromosomes* become visible in the nucleus of a cell. Chromosomes are the long, rod-like particles along which genes are arranged. *Metaphase*, the second stage of mitosis, begins when the membrane around the cell nucleus breaks down and the chromosomes move to a central band across the cell.

During *anaphase*, the third stage of mitosis, each chromosome divides in half. Each half begins to migrate to opposite ends of the cell. Finally, during *telophase*, the cell actually begins to divide into two new cells. Each new cell contains one set of chromosomes produced by the split that occurred during anaphase.

But no one knew what the role of specific molecules was in this process. Molecules were (and usually still are) too small to be seen with any microscope. Still, Watson and Crick (among others) were convinced that the answer to the puzzle of mitosis lay within the DNA molecule. So the question had become how it was that genetic information in a DNA molecule could be passed from one generation to another.

Base pairing might be a clue to answering that question. It seemed to say that anywhere an adenine occurred in a molecule, one would find a thymine paired with it (and vice versa). Also, guanine and cytosine were always paired in a DNA molecule.

Thus, knowing what a string of nitrogen bases was like in a particular DNA molecule guaranteed that one knew what the partner to that string would look like. For example, suppose a portion of a DNA molecule contained a sequence like the following:

$$- T - A - A - G - T - C - T - A - G - C - T - T - A - C -$$

What base pairing shows is that there must be another sequence of bases adjacent to this sequence that looks like this:

$$- A - T - T - C - A - G - A - T - C - G - A - A - T - G -$$

Notice how each base of the second strand is correctly paired with its partner on the first strand. Placed next to each other, the two strands would look like this:

(1) $- T - A - A - G - T - C - T - A - G - C - T - T - A - C-$
(2) $- A - T - T - C - A - G - A - T - C - G - A - A - T - G-$

But what happens if these two strands become separated from each other, as they might during cell division? Because of base pairing, each strand can act as a pattern (or "template") from which to build its partner. Notice, for example, that only one possible partner (3) can be built for strand 1, as shown below:

(1) $- T - A - A - G - T - C - T - A - G - C - T - T - A - C-$
(3) $- A - T - T - C - A - G - A - T - C - G - A - A - T - G-$

Similarly, the only possible new strand (4) that can be made from strand 2 is as follows:

(2) – A – T – T – C – A – G – A – T – C – G – A – A – T – G–
(4) – T – A – A – G – T – C – T – A – G – C – T – T – A – C–

Thus, during cell division, the original pair of base strands, (1) and (2), has divided and made two exact copies of themselves, (3) and (4).

This description goes beyond what Crick and Watson knew when they analyzed the work of Griffith and Chargaff. However, both Watson and Crick felt, at least in a general way, that base pairing might be the clue that would tie together DNA structure and the mysteries of heredity. Watson, in fact, wrote that he felt that "Chargaff's rules were a real key" in the DNA hunt.

This realization was an exciting prospect for both of them. It meant that they were one step closer to the goal of explaining nature in terms of atoms and molecules.

Crick and Watson continued to think and talk about models for DNA throughout 1952 and early 1953. They operated under one critical handicap, however. They needed—then, as always—better X-ray photographs of DNA. And there was essentially only one resource for those photographs: Maurice Wilkins's laboratory at King's College.

Wilkins was yet another scientist who had come to the hunt for DNA partly as a consequence of reading Schrodinger's *What Is Life?* Trained as a physicist, he became interested in the physical basis of living organisms. In 1946, he was invited to become a member of Sir John Randall's new biophysics unit at King's College, London.

That unit had little success at first in finding and developing successful lines of research. That was perhaps not a very surprising situation in an entirely new line of scientific investigation. Crick has written that, while there was great enthusiasm for this new line of "biophysics," no one was exactly clear as to what this field of science was, or could usefully become.

In *The Eighth Day of Creation*, Judson has observed that "Wilkins along with the rest of Randall's unit had unusual difficulty in settling on productive lines [of research]." As a result, he tended to jump from project to project, seldom getting results that encouraged him to pursue a topic further.

One of his many areas of interest was the X-ray analysis of DNA molecules. In late spring of 1950, Wilkins obtained some very pure samples of DNA at a scientific meeting. He decided to try getting X-ray photographs of the DNA. Those photographs turned out beautifully. They were the ones Watson saw in Naples in 1951, the ones that first stimulated his interest in DNA.

For a variety of reasons, Wilkins did not continue his research with DNA. That decision was ironic. As Judson has pointed out, Wilkins found himself "in the position of the inattentive lover who introduces his girl to a chance acquaintance and then must watch her stolen away." In this case, the "girl" stolen from Wilkins was the study of DNA, a topic that soon became the intellectual property of Watson and, later, Crick.

One reason for Wilkins's failure to pursue his DNA studies was that he did not feel qualified to continue this line of research. He decided that the laboratory would have to hire someone with more experience and expertise in the analysis of X-ray photographs. The person he selected was Rosalind Franklin.

Rosalind Franklin had graduated from St. Paul's Girls' School in London and Cambridge University. At the time she was hired by Wilkins, she was studying the crystal structure of coal at a laboratory in Paris. The modern field of carbon-fiber technology arose out of much of Franklin's early research.

Of all the characters described in *The Double Helix*, Rosalind Franklin is the one about whom there has been the greatest controversy. Watson's description of "Rosy," as she was called behind her back, is fairly harsh. She comes across as a cold, unfeeling, intense person with virtually no interest in her personal appearance or the impression she had on others.

Crick's assessment of Franklin was not especially complimentary either.

> *Rosalind's difficulties and her failures were mainly of her own making. Underneath her brisk manner she was oversensitive and, ironically, too determined to be scientifically sound and to avoid shortcuts. She was rather too set on succeeding all by herself and*

rather too stubborn to accept advice easily from others when it ran counter to her own ideas.

Crick blamed Rosalind's personality on her family, "who felt that scientific research was not the proper thing for a normal girl."

In the epilogue to *The Double Helix*, Watson tempered his views about Franklin who, by the time the book was published, had died. He said that he had "come to appreciate greatly her personal honesty and generosity, realizing years too late the struggles that the intelligent woman faces to be accepted by a scientific world which often regards women as mere diversions from serious thinking."

Some reviewers of *The Double Helix* took particular issue with Watson's description of Franklin. The great French microbiologist, Andre Lwoff, called Watson's remarks "cruel." "At the very least, the fact that all the work of Watson and Crick starts with Rosalind Franklin's X-ray pictures and that Jim has exploited Rosalind's results should have inclined him to indulgence," he has written.

And with regard to Watson's apparent change of heart, as provided in the epilogue to *The Double Helix*, Lwoff asks "If [his remarks] in the text were wrong, why not eliminate them?"

Another player in the DNA hunt, Erwin Chargaff, described Watson's treatment of Franklin as "merciless persiflage [joking]. I knew Miss Franklin personally . . . she was a good scientist and made crucial contributions to the understanding of the structure of DNA."

Other colleagues provided much more generous views of Franklin. They have described her as "charming," "feminine," and "outgoing," although "passionate in opinion and argument." Overall, she seems to have been remembered not so much for any particular personality traits, but as a "thoroughly professional scientist."

One of Franklin's friends, Anne Sayre, has written a book, *Rosalind Franklin and DNA*, that presents another view of Franklin and her role in the discovery of the DNA structure. Sayre begins by trying to show that Watson's description of Franklin in *The Double Helix* is misleading. He created a "character in a work of fiction [who] was not recognizable as Rosalind Franklin," she writes.

As balance to Watson's characterization of Franklin, Sayre devotes long sections of her book to explaining Franklin's true nature as a person and her accomplishments as a scientist. To describe her personality, she uses terms such as "presence," "vibrant physical energy," "striking good looks," "elegant neat swiftness," and "intensity." Franklin's professional work is described as brilliant and productive, that of one of a "select band of pioneers."

Sayre argues that Franklin was the victim of sexist attitudes among her male colleagues, especially Watson. She points out, as an example, that Franklin was not allowed to have lunch with male staff members in the "large, comfortable, rather clubby dining room" at King's College. Instead, she had to eat in the student's hall or off campus. "A minor thing," Sayre observes, "but perhaps not so very minor."

The debate over Rosalind Franklin and Watson's description of her has not been completely played out. In his 1988 account of the DNA hunt, Crick downplayed Sayre's analysis of Franklin's problems with sexism. The problems that she faced in being both a scientist and a woman, Crick thought, were "mainly trivial." "As far as I could see her colleagues treated men and women scientists alike," Crick wrote.

However one judges Franklin, it was clear that she soon became the eye of a furious storm in Wilkins's lab. Judson terms this dispute "one of the great personal quarrels in the history of science." The issue underlying the storm was what Franklin's responsibilities at the laboratory were to be.

To Wilkins, it was clear that Franklin had been hired as his assistant. Her job was to help him obtain better X-ray photographs of the DNA molecule and to interpret those photographs. To do this job, she was given the DNA samples on which Wilkins had been working, the use of the X-ray machines, and Wilkins's own assistant, a graduate student by the name of Raymond Gosling.

Franklin saw the arrangement differently. It was her understanding that the analysis of DNA was *her* problem. She had come to Wilkins's lab as a colleague, not as an assistant.

In theory, the issue should and could have been resolved as soon as Franklin arrived at King's. She did meet with John Randall, head of the biophysics unit at King's, Maurice Stokes, a physicist in the unit, and Gosling in January of 1951. But Wilkins was not present at the meeting.

The nature of Franklin's work was discussed. But Randall apparently never made it clear who had primary responsibility for DNA work in the unit. He later admitted that the meeting did not prevent some misunderstanding from developing at the very outset.

Gosling has said that Wilkins's absence from the meeting was probably critical. Had he been there, Gosling thinks, "all sorts of things might have gone differently."

Perhaps—but more than job assignments was involved in the Wilkins-Franklin quarrel. The more fundamental problem was that the two scientists "hated one another at sight." Sayre explains that

> there is no record of a relationship which began promisingly and then degenerated into hostility. Only too evidently the antipathy was instant and mutual . . . Rosalind and Wilkins were not only alienated, but hostile, and sometimes actively so.

Under the circumstances, the future course of events at King's was all too easy to predict. Within months of her arrival in London in January 1951, Franklin was refusing to share equipment and data with Wilkins. By late summer, Wilkins had decided that collaboration between himself and Franklin was impossible.

This realization did not, however, lead to any change in Wilkins's lab. Franklin had arrived on a three year fellowship. In spite of the ill will and bad feelings between her and Wilkins, the plan was for her to continue to work there for some time. And it was within that work that Watson and Crick were soon to find a critical piece of information that would lead to their solution of the DNA puzzle.

In the year following the November 1951 false start, Crick and Watson shifted their attention to matters other than DNA. They had been officially called off the topic by Bragg. And no new breaks had occurred to spur them back into their search for the DNA structure.

A major factor in this pause was the lack of better X-ray photographs. That work was still going on in Wilkins's and Franklin's labs at King's College. But Crick and Watson heard almost nothing about its results.

In late October of 1952, Crick tried to interest Watson in "having another go at the structure." But Watson saw no point in another attempt. "No fresh facts had come in to chase away the stale taste of last winter's debacle," Watson wrote. In fact, he decided, "[a]s long as Francis and I remained closed out from the experimental data," there was not much more they could do.

For most of 1952, then, Crick worked on his doctoral research. Watson became intrigued by recent discoveries that bacteria may exist in sexual forms. He spent much of his time learning more about this fascinating topic. He also appears to have had plenty of time for vacations, parties, and other forms of relaxation.

This lull came to an abrupt conclusion in January of 1953 when Watson and Crick received the copy of Pauling's paper describing his DNA model. They immediately decided that Wilkins would have to be told about the paper.

Watson and Crick were still officially prohibited from working on DNA. But they hoped that the news about Pauling's paper would change all that. Only a month earlier, Watson had expressed the hope that "the urgency created by Linus' assault on DNA might make him [Wilkins] ask Francis and me for help."

But they had received no such encouragement from Wilkins. Watson did learn that Franklin was leaving King's College at the end of the term and, at that point, that Wilkins planned to resume his own research on DNA.

But in January, time was even more critical. Watson and Crick needed to get back to work on DNA as soon as possible. Since Watson was planning to visit London soon anyway, he arranged to see Wilkins on January 30.

When Watson arrived at King's College, he found Wilkins busy. So he decided to stop in Franklin's office to show her the Pauling paper. What follows has become a classic tale in science. Unfortunately, we have only one participant's view of the drama that unfolded—Watson's. Franklin left no written record of the events.

Watson claims in *The Double Helix* that his news about Pauling's paper upset Franklin terribly. He explains that he tried to point out how similar Pauling's triple helix model was to their own

(Watson and Crick's) failed model of November 1951. But as Watson pursued this line of discussion, Franklin only "became increasingly annoyed."

Watson felt sure that it was his insistence on talking about helices that disturbed Franklin so much. She became so distraught, he wrote, that "she was hardly able to control her temper." Watson based his description on the belief that Franklin had long been insisting that DNA could not exist as a helix.

Another view of this controversy is presented by Sayre, who claims that Watson "persistently muddle[d] Rosalind's opinion concerning the helical nature of the B form (yes, it was) with her more tentative opinion concerning the A form (it might or might not be)."

In fact, Franklin probably had other good reasons for becoming angry at Watson's news. For nearly a year, she had been corresponding with Robert Corey, Pauling's coauthor on the DNA paper. It must have seemed something of an insult to her that Watson, who was not working on DNA at the time, had received a copy of the paper when she, who was working on it, did not.

Watson goes on to describe how he was attacked by Franklin. He later wrote that he feared that "in her hot anger she might strike me." Watson was saved from any physical assault, however, by Wilkins's appearance in the room.

The scene, dramatic as it might have been, also contains an element of humor. Franklin may, indeed, have been ready to attack Watson. But Watson was hardly in much danger. As Judson reminds us, Franklin was short and slim and Watson over six feet tall.

The real drama surrounding Watson's visit had not ended when he and Wilkins left Franklin's lab. As the two men walked up the hallway, Wilkins mentioned to Watson that Franklin had been making important progress in her DNA photography. Most important had been her discovery that DNA existed in two forms, which she called "A" and "B."

Judson points out in *The Eighth Day of Creation* how remarkable this piece of news was. Franklin had made the discovery of the A and B forms more than a year earlier. Wilkins, Watson and Crick had been in constant communication by letter and in person throughout that year.

Yet, for whatever reason, Wilkins had apparently never mentioned the B structure to Watson or Crick. At least, Watson claims that his January 30 visit to King's was the first time he had heard about this form of DNA.

So, when Wilkins now mentioned the B structure, Watson asked if a photograph of the B form was available. At that point, Wilkins revealed that he had secretly been making copies of Franklin's photographs. She had made arrangements to have her fellowship transferred to another laboratory, that of Desmond Bernal at Birkbeck College. Wilkins wanted to be sure that he would have copies of the work Franklin did at King's after she left.

Thus, Watson had his first look at the now famous "photograph 51." That photograph is the one shown on page 7 of this book. Franklin had taken the photograph in May of 1952. It was by far the clearest photograph of DNA yet obtained. She had immediately seen the potential value in the photograph. But she did not begin a study of it. Instead, she decided to finish her analysis of the A photographs on which she was then working.

A number of reasons lay behind that decision. For one thing, the A form was more crystalline than the B form and, hence, likely to produce better photographs. Also, since the A and B forms were obviously related to each other structurally, it made some sense to concentrate on the form for which the greater amount of data already existed, the A form.

Thus, in her careful, orderly way, Franklin decided to complete her analysis of the A form before going on to the B form. That analysis took the better part of a year.

When Watson had his first look at photograph 51, his reaction was immediate. "The instant I saw the picture," he writes, "my mouth fell open and my pulse began to race."

The reason for Watson's excitement was the clarity of photograph 51. It left absolutely no doubt that the DNA molecule was a helix. Until that point, no one had been able to rule out a non-helical structure for DNA. Franklin had reminded her colleagues about this point on more than one occasion.

The basis for this uncertainty had been the A photographs, always too unclear to allow a definite decision to be made about the molecule's structure. But the B photograph was another matter. Watson writes that

> the pattern was unbelievably simpler than those obtained previously [from the A form]. Moreover, the black cross of reflections which dominated the picture could arise only from a helical structure.

Watson was convinced that a brief study of the X-ray photograph would reveal the major characteristics of the molecule.

At dinner with Wilkins that evening, Watson tried to find out what else the King's group may have learned about the characteristics of the DNA molecule. Had they made more calculations that would provide the spacing between atoms and the number of chains, for example?

He was not very successful. Watson writes that

> Since Maurice's long-drawn-out reply never came to the point, I could not decide whether he was saying that no one at King's had measured the pertinent reflections or whether he wanted to eat his meal before it got cold.

Perhaps the most concrete result of Watson's visit to London was his decision to reconsider a two-chain model. He recognized that he and others may have become stuck on the three-chain concept. And it was now clear from photograph 51 that a two-chain model could not be ruled out.

On his train ride back to Cambridge, Watson sketched all he could remember of photograph 51. The next day, he told Bragg, Kendrew, and Crick of his discovery. Bragg realized that he could no longer prevent Crick and Watson from working on the DNA problem. He gave them permission to begin another model building attempt.

The next effort got under way with a substantial amount of information already in hand. First, the evidence from photograph 51 seemed to point almost certainly to some type of helical structure. Second, earlier X-ray photos by William Astbury had shown that the distance between bases in the molecule was 3.4 angstroms (1 angstrom = 10^{-10} meter or about 4×10^{-9} inch).

Third, Astbury's photos also gave the repeat distance in the molecule, the vertical distance required for one complete turn of the helix. Finally, Wilkins's research had provided a value of 20 angstroms for the diameter of the molecule.

Thus, only three major questions remained to be solved about the DNA structure. First, how many helices did the molecule contain? Second, were the nitrogen bases on the inside or the outside of the molecule? Third, how were the bases arranged in relationship to each other? The last question was especially critical if the decision was made to place the bases on the inside of the molecule.

The next five weeks were hectic times. Work was slow at first because Watson and Crick did not have the correct jigs for the model. Both went back to other work briefly while the machine shop kept busy turning out models of nitrogen bases, sugars, and phosphate groups.

When the model parts were ready, Watson began assembling a two-chain structure with the sugar-phosphate backbone on the inside. He worked for more than two days without much success. Watson reports that the results were "even more unsatisfactory than our three-chained models of fifteen months before."

Watson was doing the actual work on the model, while Crick sat nearby at his desk, working on his thesis. From time to time, Crick looked up and commented on Watson's work. After seeing Watson's lack of success with the two-chain model, Crick finally asked Watson why he didn't put the bases on the inside of the model, instead of on the outside.

Watson had one good scientific reason for not doing so. Having the bases on the outside of the molecule would have made them readily available to other parts of the cell. That way, whatever genetic instructions they carried could easily be "read" by the cell.

But Watson had another objection to putting the bases inside. Doing so would introduce a new problem of deciding how the bases would be arranged in relationship to each other. On the outside of the molecule, each base could stick out from the backbone without any special relationship to other bases.

On the inside, bases on each chain would be in close proximity to bases on the other chain. Watson would have to decide how to arrange the bases in order to satisfy all necessary chemical forces.

Watson hesitated to take on this challenge, he says, because he feared that "it would be possible to build an almost infinite number of models of this type." And he didn't think there would be any way of knowing which of this infinite number was the correct one.

But Watson finally decided that the effort had to be made. So he was soon building two-chain models with the bases on the inside and the sugar-phosphate backbone on the outside. As expected, the arrangement of bases created the most difficult problem. At first, he tried like-with-like arrangements, adenine with guanine and cytosine with thymine. As Figure 8 (page 48) shows, adenine and guanine are "like" bases since they are both double-ring relatives of purines. Similarly, cytosine and thymine are single-ring relatives of pyrimidine.

This arrangement was unsatisfactory, because it caused the molecule to bulge in some places (where the purines were paired) and to constrict at other places (where the pyrimidines were paired). And Crick and Watson knew that the molecule had to have the same diameter everywhere.

This problem is all the more remarkable since both Watson and Crick already had the exact clue they needed to solve this problem. They had been familiar with the Chargaff ratios and the calculations performed by John Griffith for at least six months. Yet, both somehow ignored these data. Gribbin says that the two proceeded "with almost obstinate blindness to the significance" of these two crucial pieces of information.

Eventually Watson realized that his like-with-like model was a hopeless effort. So he started building an "unlike" model, with a thymine on one chain, opposite an adenine on the opposite chain, and with guanines and cytosines opposite each other. Almost at once, he saw that this model would work. He explained that

> Suddenly I became aware that an adenine-thymine pair held together by two hydrogen bonds was identical in shape to a guanine-cytosine pair held together by at least two hydrogen bonds. All the hydrogen bonds seemed to form naturally; no fudging was required to make the two types of base pairs identical in shape.

(The hydrogen bonds that Watson mentions here are weak chemical bonds that occur in many biological molecules, including DNA.)

The date was Saturday, March 7, 1953. The DNA puzzle had apparently been solved. The model would still have to pass inspection by colleagues at Cavendish and at King's. But Watson was convinced that this time they had the correct answer. Still, he confessed to being somewhat uneasy when Crick left the laboratory and "winged into the Eagle to tell everyone within hearing distance that we had found the secret of life."

Over the next two weeks, almost everyone with the remotest interest in DNA passed through Watson and Crick's lab. Bragg, Perutz, Kendrew, Donahue, Wilkins, Franklin, and Gosling all

Watson and Crick in front of their correct model of DNA in March of 1953.
(Cold Spring Harbor Laboratory Library Archives)

gave their approval to what they saw. Watson and Crick began writing a report of their work and a description of their model. That report was published on April 25, 1953, as a short letter to ↚ the journal *Nature*. The letter began, "We wish to suggest a structure for the salt of deoxyribose nucleic acid (D.N.A.). This structure has novel features which are of considerable biological interest." The model that was described in this letter is shown in Figure 9.

The accomplishment by Watson and Crick had been a brilliant one. They certainly had made errors along the way. They had misunderstood or ignored valuable tips from Franklin, Chargaff, Griffith, and others in the months before they got the right answer. They often knew less science—crystallography and chemistry, in particular—than they might have. They sometimes used methods (as with Rosalind Franklin's data) that were ethically dubious.

But, perhaps more important, they brought just the right combination of intellectual and personality traits to their search for DNA. They were absolutely committed to their work. They had found a way to combine physical and biological perspectives in their research. They were willing to look at problems in a new and different way. They both—but especially Watson—had an ability to look at the problem they were working on from the broadest possible perspective.

Finally, they seemed to work almost perfectly together. Gribbin has pointed out that

> *The great thing they had going for them was that, as a team, they could bounce ideas off each other, pulling each other's notions to bits and rebuilding them as necessary.*

He goes on to point out that this interaction between two brilliant minds was precisely what was lacking at King's where Wilkins and Franklin were not only unable to work together but were also "scarcely on speaking terms."

The reward that came to Watson and Crick was the discovery of the structure of one of the most remarkable molecules ever studied. That DNA molecule was perhaps best described by Watson a short time after the discovery. In a somewhat bleary-eyed state after an evening of food and drink, he managed to say of the DNA molecule, "It's so beautiful, you see, so beautiful!"

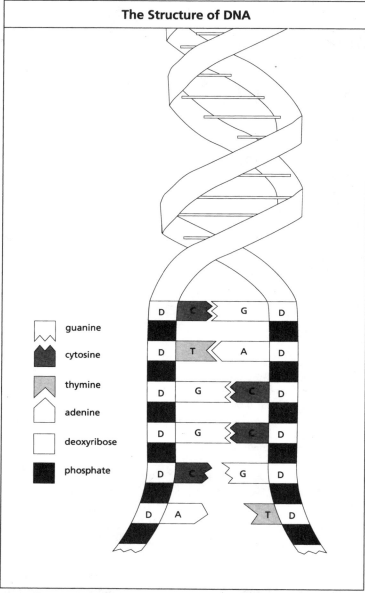

The Structure of DNA

guanine

cytosine

thymine

adenine

deoxyribose

phosphate

Figure 9: In their 1953 letter to *Nature*, Watson and Crick described the model for the structure of DNA as shown in this diagram. The specifics of replication, however, were worked out later.

A "space-filling" model of the DNA molecule that shows the relative position of the atoms in the molecule. (USDA, photo by George Everett)

And, of course, it was. It was the realization of both Watson and Crick's dreams; a physical representation of that elusive key to heredity—the gene.

CHAPTER 4 NOTES

p. 44   "We weren't working very hard . . ." Horace Freeland Judson, *The Eighth Day of Creation* (New York: Simon and Schuster, 1979), p. 91.

p. 46   "If a student . . ." James Watson, *The Double Helix* (New York: Atheneum, 1968), p. 161.

p. 49   "Well, of course . . ." Robert Olby, *The Path to the Double Helix* (Seattle University of Washington Press, 1974), p. 388.

p. 49   "never met two men . . ." Judson, *The Eighth Day*, p. 143.

p. 51   "Chargaff's rules . . ." Watson, *Double Helix*, p. 144.

pp. 52–53   "Rosalind's difficulties . . ." Francis Crick, "How to Live with a Golden Helix," *The Sciences* (September, 1979): p. 7.

p. 53   "At the very least . . ." Andre Lwoff, "Truth, truth," *Scientific American* (July 1968): p. 136.

p. 53   "merciless persiflage . . ." Erwin Chargaff, "A Quick Climb up Mount Olympus," *Science* (March 29, 1968): p. 1449.

p. 53   "charming," etc. Judson, *The Eighth Day*, pp. 147–48.

p. 55   "all sorts of things . . ." Judson, *The Eighth Day*, p 103–04.

p. 55   "hated one another . . ." Sayre, *Rosalind Franklin and DNA* (New York: Norton, 1975), p. 95.

p. 56   "having another go . . ." Watson, *Double Helix*, pp. 145, 148.

p. 56   "the urgency . . ." Judson, *The Eighth Day*, p. 154.

p. 57   "in her hot anger . . ." Watson, *Double Helix*, p. 166.

p. 58   "The instant . . ." Watson, *Double Helix*, p. 167.

p. 59   "The pattern . . ." Watson, *Double Helix*, p. 169.

p. 59   "Since Maurice . . ." Watson, *Double Helix*, pp. 170–71.

p. 60   "even more unsatisfactory . . ." Watson, *Double Helix*, p. 177.

p. 61   "it would be possible . . ." Watson, *Double Helix*, p. 177.

p. 61   "Suddenly I became . . ." Watson, *Double Helix*, pp. 194–96.

p. 62   "winged into the Eagle . . ." Watson, *Double Helix*, p. 197.

p. 63   "The great thing . . ." Gribbin, *In Search of the Double Helix* (Aldershot, England: Wildwood House, 1985), p. 227.

p. 63   "It's so beautiful . . ." Crick, "How to Live," p. 9.

5

NEW BEGINNINGS

Watson and Crick's discovery marked the end of a long search to find the structure of the DNA molecule. It concluded what one scientist has called "the greatest achievement of science in the 20th century" and another has called "the adventure story of science in the 20th century."

But solving the DNA puzzle was anything but the end of their careers for those involved in the story. After all, Watson was only 23 years old, less than two years out of graduate school. Crick had not even earned his doctoral degree, although he did so within a matter of months.

Both Watson and Crick had brilliant careers ahead of them. Watson left Cambridge in the fall of 1953 to become a senior research fellow at the California Institute of Technology. Then, in 1955, he moved to Harvard, where he remained for the next 21 years. In 1969, he also became director of the Cold Spring Harbor Laboratory of Quantitative Biology. He has served on a number of government committees and, most recently, was appointed director of the Human Genome Project at the National Institutes of Health.

In addition to *The Double Helix*, Watson has written a textbook that has become a modern classic in its field, *The Molecular Biology of the Gene*. Also, in 1968, at the age of 39, he married a 19-year-old Radcliffe College student, Elizabeth Lewis, who was working in his laboratory. They have two sons, Rufus and Duncan.

Crick spent the 1953–54 academic year with the Protein Structure Project at Brooklyn Polytechnic Institute. He returned to Cambridge in 1954 and remained on the faculty there until 1976.

From left to right, Anne Cullis, Francis Crick, Don Caspar, Aaron Klug, Rosalind Franklin, Odile Crick, John Kendrew at scientific meeting in Madrid in 1956. (Medical Research Council Laboratory of Molecular Biology, courtesy Dr. Don Caspar)

He eventually became codirector (with Sydney Brenner) of the Cell Biology Division of the Medical Research Council Laboratory.

During these years he was also visiting professor at the Rockefeller Institute (1959) and at Harvard University (1959 and 1962). In 1977, Crick accepted an appointment at the Salk Institute for Biological Studies in La Jolla, California, where he has remained ever since.

Crick has written three books. *Of Molecules and Men* (1966) outlines his arguments against the theory of vitalism. *Life Itself: Its Origin and Nature* (1981) explains Crick's theories about the origins of life elsewhere in the universe. *What Mad Pursuit* (1988) is an autobiography that provides his view of the events that led to the discovery of the double helix.

In 1962, Watson, Crick, and Maurice Wilkins were awarded the Nobel Prize in medicine or physiology for their work on the DNA molecule.

Wilkins continued his work on X-ray diffraction analysis at King's College. With two colleagues, he published a paper supporting the Watson-Crick model of DNA in the same issue of *Nature*. Since 1955, Wilkins has been professor of molecular biology and deputy director of the Biophysical Research Unit of the Medical Research Council at King's College.

Wilkins spent some time working in the field of neurobiology, the study of nerve cells and nervous systems. He did some research on the membranes of nerve cells but found that the work was "not very interesting." He was never able to "find a suitable line of work which was really interesting," so he gave up this field of research after a while.

Instead, he has spent much of his time working on broader issues involving the social implications of science: food and famine, nuclear disarmament, and the social responsibilities of scientists, for example.

Wilkins has been somewhat critical of the reductionist positions taken by both Crick and Watson. (The ideas of reductionism were explained on page xii of this book.) He feels that their ideas that "everything about life and human beings can be explained in terms of atoms and molecules" is wrong. He thinks that, although molecular biology has been a powerful scientific tool, it is never going to give scientists the ability to comprehend everything about the world.

Rosalind Franklin had, by the time of the Watson-Crick discovery, moved to Birkbeck College. She and Gosling also added a paper in support of the double helix model in the same issue of *Nature*.

Her career was, however, to be tragically short. She died of cancer at the age of 37 in April 1958. She had been diagnosed with the disease only months before her death. Yet, even after a hospital stay, she continued to work in her laboratory, almost until her death.

There has been much debate about the role that Rosalind Franklin played in the discovery of DNA. Her photograph 51 was obviously an important key to solving the puzzle. Yet, of the four people most closely involved with research on the DNA puzzle (Watson, Crick, Wilkins, and herself), only she was not included in the Nobel Prize.

One reason is that the rules for Nobel Prizes specify that no more than three individuals may be included in any one award. Also, the prize can be awarded only to living scientists. When the award for the DNA discovery was given in 1962, Franklin had already been dead for four years.

Nonetheless, some critics have argued that she deserved more recognition than she has received. J. D. Bernal, the great crystallographer and Franklin's superior at Birkbeck College, has written that he would have been shocked if Franklin had not received a share of the prize, had she lived.

Others, including Anne Sayre, have pondered the possibility that the prize might have been split only two ways, between Watson and Crick, or with Franklin in place of Wilkins.

More important than the loss of the Nobel Prize, Sayre believes, is all of the other recognition Franklin had earned, but not received. She calls this loss "slow and gentle robbery" by scientists who could and should have acknowledged her achievements, but who have not done so.

John Gribbin has presented an even stronger, more comprehensive, criticism of the way credit for the DNA discovery was handled. He points out that, in their April 25, 1953, paper in *Nature*, Watson and Crick failed to give adequate recognition to Franklin, Wilkins, and Gosling, whose work had been instrumental in their discovery. He claims that the three papers that appeared together—one by Watson and Crick, one by Wilkins and two other colleagues at King's, and one by Franklin and Gosling—give a completely false history of the way the DNA structure was actually determined.

"Nobody could have guessed from this presentation," Gribbin writes, "that the type B photograph had actually been the inspiration for Watson's final attack on the problem." Instead, the papers seem to suggest that the model "sprang, as a stroke of inspiration, from Watson's and Crick's basic knowledge of chemistry, not from any detailed X-ray data." That view of events, of course, would be quite incorrect.

Watson and Crick's colleagues at Cambridge, John Kendrew and Max Perutz, were also awarded Nobel Prizes in 1962. Their awards were given in chemistry for their research on the structure of the protein.

Appearing in Stockholm with Watson, Crick, Wilkins, Kendrew, and Perutz was Linus Pauling. Pauling was there to receive his second Nobel Prize, the peace award. He continued to be a major figure in science and politics for the next three decades.

CHAPTER 5 NOTES

p. 67   "the greatest achievement . . ." Peter Medawar and Jacob Bronowski, respectively, as quoted in Kendrick Frazier, "Twists in the Double Helix," *Science News* (June 15, 1974): p. 388.

p. 69   "not very interesting," etc. Stephanie Johnson and Thomas R. Mertens, "An Interview with Nobel Laureate Maurice Wilkins," *American Biology Teacher* (March 1989): pp. 151–53.

p. 71   "sprang as a stroke . . ." John Gribbin, *In Search of the Double Helix* (Aldershot, England: Wildwood House, 1985), p. 243.

6

FRANCIS CRICK:
THE LATER YEARS

Any good scientific model has two characteristics. First, it ties together and explains many facts already known to scientists. Second, it raises many new questions and problems and suggests new lines of research. To the extent that those questions and problems lead to interesting new results, the model is a good one.

In this respect, the Watson-Crick model of DNA has turned out to be one of the most powerful models in the history of biology, if not of all science. The model suggested how two of the most important of all questions in biology might be answered: How do replication and protein synthesis occur?

Replication is the process by which a cell divides into two parts. Each of the two new cells is normally identical to the parent cell. When a hair cell divides, for example, it produces two new hair cells, both (normally) identical to the original cell. How does it happen that the process of replication occurs so perfectly?

The Watson-Crick model of DNA provided an easy and obvious answer to that question. The process by which each strand of a DNA molecule can make an exact copy of itself was described on pages 50–52. The DNA molecule opens up to expose the nitrogen bases. Each strand of DNA then acts like a template from which a new strand can be made. The order of bases on the new strand is dictated by the sequence of bases on the old strand. Eventually, two new DNA molecules are produced. Both are (usually) exact copies of the original molecule.

No one understood the details of this process in 1953. For example, some critics of the Watson-Crick model pointed out that the two strands of the double helix were tightly wrapped around each other. They would have to untangle and separate before replication could occur. It was not clear how this process could take place.

Crick and Watson understood this problem and others that critics raised about the model. In fact, they discussed them in some detail in a paper in *Nature* published late in 1953. But they were also convinced that the general idea described by their model was so clear and so obvious that it had to be true. The problem now was to find the mechanism by which replication actually took place.

Their confidence in the DNA model was confirmed only four years later when Matthew Meselson and Franklin Stahl reported on their experiments that explained the steps that occurred when replication took place.

The second avenue of research suggested by the Watson-Crick model—on protein synthesis—was much more complex. All scientists acknowledge the critical role of proteins in living organisms. Crick himself once said that "proteins can do almost anything" in a living organism.

Once the structure of DNA was determined, the question became how the genetic instructions stored in a DNA molecule could be used to direct the manufacture of a new protein molecule.

That question really has two parts. First, how can a genetic message be stored in a DNA molecule? Second, how can that message be translated into a protein molecule?

Both Crick and Watson had thought about these questions before they found the structure of DNA. The answer to the first question seemed apparent. The sugar-phosphate backbone could not be involved in the genetic message. Every DNA molecule had exactly the same sugar-phosphate backbone. So the backbone could not provide any special information to a cell.

The genetic information must be stored in the nitrogen bases. The arrangement of these bases in the DNA molecule must somehow code for various genetic traits, such as hair and eye color, and handedness (left or right).

After the 1953 discovery, Crick spent more than a decade working on the details of this problem. He summarized this coding problem in a speech before the Symposium of the Society for Experimental Biology in September of 1957. In that speech he announced his "sequence hypothesis." (A hypothesis is an idea that has not yet been proven true.) That hypothesis was that the sequence of bases in a DNA molecule "is a (simple) code for the amino acid sequence of a particular protein."

The problem was straightforward. DNA contains four nitrogen bases: adenine, cytosine, guanine, and thymine. Protein molecules are, at their most simple level, long strings of units called amino acids. Human proteins are made of 20 different amino acids. Examples of these acids are glycine, alanine, proline, phenylalanine, and glutamic acid. The question is how can four nitrogen bases in DNA be used to carry instructions, or code, for making 20 different amino acids?

There are different sorts of codes. In one kind of code, numbers can stand for letters. For example, the number 1 can stand for A, 2 for B, 3 for C, and so on. But this system would not work as the DNA code. There are only four "numbers," that is four nitrogen bases, to use in the code. So the code would be able to give only four "letters," that is, four amino acids.

Another possibility is to use just four numbers, but use them in combination. For example, use the numbers 1, 2, 3, and 4 in combinations of two. Then the number 11 could stand for A, 12 for B, 13 for C, 14 for D, 21 for E, 22 for F, and so on. But using the numbers to code in this way, there are only 16 different combinations, hence 16 different letters. Thus, taking two nitrogen bases at a time would still not provide a code for 20 different amino acids.

It took dozens of scientists working more than a decade to unravel this problem. Sometimes they worked with DNA and sometimes with ribonucleic acid (RNA), another kind of nucleic acid. RNA also contains four nitrogen bases, but they are slightly different from those in DNA. Like DNA, RNA contains adenine, cytosine, and guanine, but it contains *uracil* (U) in place of the thymine found in DNA.

Crick was one of those who tried a variety of different ideas. Most of the time he tried to think through the answer to the problem. He studied the results of many experiments and tried to figure out what they meant. He proposed new theories for others to test out in the laboratory.

At one point, however, he decided to do some laboratory research himself—the kind of work he enjoyed most. He was not very good at actual hands-on experiments. One coworker wrote that "He's just not very practical; he would drive a microscope eyepiece right through the slide—very unhandy." Nonetheless, he worked very hard in the laboratory, often coming in weekends to finish his experiments.

Eventually scientists began to unravel the code. The first breakthrough came in 1961. An American biochemist, Marshall Nirenberg, discovered that a set of three nitrogen bases in RNA, UUU, coded for the amino acid phenylalanine. That discovery meant that every time a cell sees the sequence UUU on an RNA molecule, it "knows" that it must make a phenylalanine molecule.

It had become clear that a set of three bases was needed to code for each amino acid. This set of bases was called a *codon*. Over the next six years, scientists discovered the codons for all 20 amino acids. This information is now called the genetic code.

The table in Figure 10 was first proposed by Crick. It shows the codons for each amino acid. To use the table, read down the left side first, then across the top, then down the right side. To find the meaning of the codon GCA, for example, first read down the left column until you come to "G." Then read across the top until you come to "C." Then read down the column until you find the letter "A." The amino acid corresponding to this codon is "Ala," which stands for the amino acid alanine.

Notice that three spaces in the table are marked as "stop." These three spaces represent codons that code for *no* amino acid. Scientists found that these codons carry a different set of instructions. They tell a cell when to stop making a protein molecule. It was fitting that the last of these three "stop" codes was identified by Crick, working with Sydney Brenner, in 1967.

In addition, one codon tells a cell when to start making a protein. That codon is AUG, which also codes for the amino acid methionine (Met). The process of making a protein always begins with methionine.

The Genetic Code

Second base

First base		U		C		A		G		Third base
		U		C		A		G		
U		UUU	Phe	UCU	Ser	UAU	Tyr	UGU	Cys	U
		UUC	Phe	UCC	Ser	UAC	Tyr	UGC	Cys	C
		UUA	Leu	UCA	Ser	UAA	Stop	UGA	Stop	A
		UUG	Leu	UCG	Ser	UAG	Stop	UGG	Trp	G
C		CUU	Leu	CCU	Pro	CAU	His	CGU	Arg	U
		CUC	Leu	CCC	Pro	CAC	His	CGC	Arg	C
		CUA	Leu	CCA	Pro	CAA	Gln	CGA	Arg	A
		CUG	Leu	CCG	Pro	CAG	Gln	CGG	Arg	G
A		AUU	Ile	ACU	Thr	AAU	Asn	AGU	Ser	U
		AUC	Ile	ACC	Thr	AAC	Asn	AGC	Ser	C
		AUA	Ile	ACA	Thr	AAA	Lys	AGA	Arg	A
		AUG	Met (start)	ACG	Thr	AAG	Lys	AGG	Arg	G
G		GUU	Val	GCU	Ala	GAU	Asp	GGU	Gly	U
		GUC	Val	GCC	Ala	GAC	Asp	GGC	Gly	C
		GUA	Val	GCA	Ala	GAA	Glu	GGA	Gly	A
		GUG	Val	GCG	Ala	GAG	Glu	GGG	Gly	G

The genetic code given above is for RNA.

The amino acid abbreviations in the code are as follows:

Phe: phenylalanine	His: histidine
Leu: leucine	Gln: glutamine
Ile: isoleucine	Asn: aspargine
Met: methionine	Lys: lysine
Val: valine	Asp: aspartic acid
Ser: serine	Glu: glutamic acid
Pro: proline	Cys: cysteine
Thr: threonine	Trp: tryptophan
Ala: alanine	Arg: arginine
Tyr: tyrosine	Gly: glycine

Figure 10

Studies of the genetic code always went hand-in-hand with the second big problem of protein synthesis: How was the code used to make new proteins? After all, DNA is present in the nucleus of cells. Protein is made *outside* the nucleus, in ribosomes. Ribosomes are small structures in a cell's cytoplasm. How did the message stored in DNA get transferred from the nucleus to the location in the cell where it was actually used, the ribosomes?

Watson and Crick had both thought about that question early on. They had similar ideas as to how the process might work. They did not believe that DNA could make protein directly. Instead, they thought that the coded message in DNA was first transferred to the second type of nucleic acid molecule, RNA. Then, the RNA was used to make protein. As early as November of 1952, Watson had made a sketch that showed how he thought the process might work.

Crick continued working on this problem for many years. In his paper for the Society of Experimental Biology in 1957, he also explained how he thought protein synthesis could occur. That idea can be described in a diagram like the one in Figure 11. In this diagram, solid arrows stand for methods by which information is *probably* transferred. Dotted arrows stand for pathways by which information *might* be transferred. The absence of an arrow represents a process by which information is probably *not* transferred.

The circular arrow around DNA stands for replication. It means that genetic information in one DNA molecule can be passed to other DNA molecules (by replication). Crick thought that a similar process might be possible with RNA molecules. One RNA molecule might be able to make a copy of itself in making a new RNA molecule. This is shown by the circular arrow around RNA.

The production of protein was most likely to occur, Crick thought, when DNA molecules copied their information into RNA molecules (the solid line from DNA to RNA in Figure 11). That information was then used by RNA molecules to make proteins (the solid arrow from RNA to protein in the figure). Because these RNA molecules carry the genetic message from DNA to proteins, they are now known as messenger RNA (mRNA) molecules. Crick named this idea the Central Dogma.

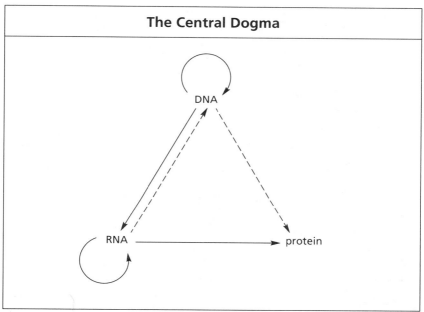

The Central Dogma

DNA

RNA → protein

Figure 11: Shown above is Crick's explanation of the way genetic information is passed through the molecules in a cell, which he called the Central Dogma. He felt that protein production was most likely to occur when DNA molecules copied their information into RNA, which then made proteins. Numerous experiments since have proven this to be correct.

Some scientists strongly disagreed with this idea. They were not convinced that DNA alone was "the master molecule." One biologist, Barry Commoner, wrote that replication and protein synthesis were much more complicated than Crick's diagram suggested. He claimed that the manufacture of proteins depended not on DNA, "but a multi-molecular system which is so complex as to require the participation of the entire living cell."

Crick did not disagree that protein synthesis was complex. But he insisted that DNA was always the original source of information, never protein. He said many times that the flow of information in cells was always from DNA to protein and that "once 'information' has passed into protein it *cannot get out again* . . . [that is] transfer from protein to protein or from protein to nucleic acid is impossible."

Time has proven Crick to be correct. No single experiment has confirmed the Central Dogma. Great scientific ideas usually do not work that way. Instead, thousands and thousands of experiments have been done, assuming that the Central Dogma is true. Every time one of those experiments works out as expected, scientists are a little more confident that the Central Dogma is correct.

Today, scientists know that Crick's general idea was incomplete in some respects. But overall, it was an accurate representation of the chemical changes that take place in cells. It has come to be accepted as one of the great theories of modern biology.

The synthesis of proteins in cells is now recognized as a two-stage process. In the first stage, the genetic message stored in DNA is transcribed into messenger RNA (mRNA) molecules. This stage begins when a segment of the DNA molecule unravels, exposing its nitrogen bases. Then, the sequence of nitrogen bases along that strand is used to manufacture a new mRNA molecule.

Suppose that the exposed strand looks like this:

$$- D - P - D - P - D - P - D - P - D - P - D - P - D - P - D -$$

$$|\quad\quad|\quad\quad|\quad\quad|\quad\quad|\quad\quad|\quad\quad|\quad\quad|$$

$$T\quad\quad C\quad\quad G\quad\quad C\quad\quad A\quad\quad T\quad\quad T\quad\quad C$$

In this diagram, the "D" stands for the sugar deoxyribose, the "P" for the phosphate group, and "A," "C," "G," and "T" for the four nitrogen bases.

The mRNA molecule that is made from this strand, then, has the following structure:

$$- R - P - R - P - R - P - R - P - R - P - R - P - R - P - R -$$

$$|\quad\quad|\quad\quad|\quad\quad|\quad\quad|\quad\quad|\quad\quad|\quad\quad|$$

$$A\quad\quad G\quad\quad C\quad\quad G\quad\quad U\quad\quad A\quad\quad A\quad\quad G$$

The backbone of the mRNA molecule contains the sugar ribose (R) instead of deoxyribose and the phosphate group (P). The nitrogen bases in the mRNA strand are determined by the base-pairing rule. For example, the first T in the DNA molecule dictates that the first base in the mRNA molecule must be an A. The next DNA base, a C, dictates a G in the mRNA molecule. And so on.

The one exception is that thymine (T) does not occur in RNA. Instead, uracil (U) occurs wherever one would expect to find thymine. For an RNA molecule, the base-pairing rules are: adenine (A) pairs with uracil (U), and guanine (G) pairs with cytosine (C). Thus, the fifth DNA base, A, dictates the placement of a U in the corresponding position in the mRNA molecule.

When the new mRNA molecule has been completed, it leaves the nucleus and goes into the cytoplasm. There it attaches itself to a ribosome. The ribosome moves down the mRNA molecule, from one end to the other. As it moves down the molecule, it "reads" the sequence of nitrogen bases, one codon at a time.

For each codon it reads, the ribosome locates the correct amino acid corresponding to that codon. For example, the first codon in the mRNA molecule above is AGC. That sequence of nitrogen bases codes for the amino acide serine (Ser). When the ribosome passes over that codon, it will position a serine molecule next to the mRNA.

As each codon is read, another amino acid is brought into position. The new amino acid bonds to the other amino acids already present next to the mRNA molecule. Eventually, a long chain of amino acids—a new protein—has been constructed. The exact sequence of amino acids has been dictated by the sequence of nitrogen bases in the mRNA molecule which, in turn, was dictated by the base sequence in the cell's DNA.

Crick was interested in a third problem relating to protein synthesis: adapter molecules. Chemists can look at an amino acid molecule and an mRNA molecule and see one thing: The two kinds of molecules cannot fit next to each other. Complex biochemical forces keep them apart. But that presents a problem. How can an mRNA molecule make a protein molecule if mRNA and amino acids cannot get near each other?

Crick thought he knew the answer to that question. He proposed the idea that cells contain special kinds of molecules that act like adapters. An adapter molecule is one, he said, that can hold an amino acid at one end and that can attach to an mRNA molecule at the opposite end. The inset in Figure 12 shows what an adapter molecule might look like.

If such molecules existed, one could see how protein synthesis might occur. Figure 12 illustrates the complete process of protein

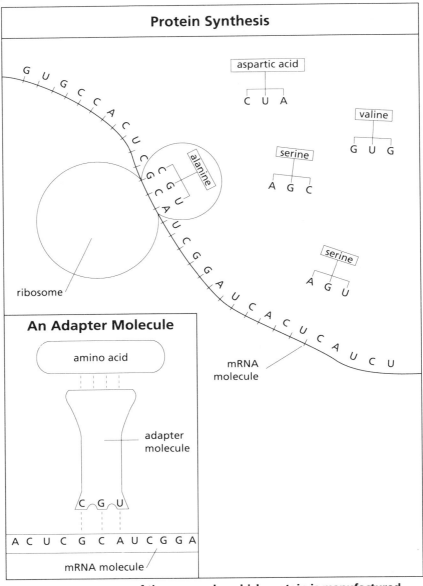

Figure 12: A summary of the process by which protein is manufactured is shown above. (Inset) Crick first suggested the idea of an adapter molecule early in 1955. Numerous experiments done during the following years proved Crick correct. Adapter molecules are now known as transfer RNA (tRNA).

synthesis. This figure shows an mRNA molecule attached to a ribosome in a cell. Some adapter molecules are also shown. Each adapter molecule holds a different amino acid. Crick said that there would have to be 20 different kinds of adapter molecules in a cell because there are 20 different amino acids.

Adapter molecules eventually find their way to the mRNA molecule. They hook on to the mRNA at their free ends, next to the appropriate codons. When they do so, the amino acids at their opposite ends are lined up next to each other. Then the amino acids join together, and a protein is formed. After the protein is made, the adapter molecules break loose from the protein and the mRNA.

Crick first suggested his idea for adapter molecules in a letter to the RNA Tie Club in early 1955. The RNA Tie Club was an informal group of scientists created by George Gamow. Gamow, a theoretical physicist, had come to the United States from his native Russia in 1933. He was interested in a great many different subjects, among which were the genetic code and protein synthesis.

In 1954, Gamow created the RNA Tie Club. Its purpose, he said, was "to solve the riddle of RNA structure, and to understand the way it builds proteins." He designed a tie with the club's symbol, an RNA molecule with a green sugar-phosphate chain and yellow bases. He planned to select 20 members for the club, one for each amino acid.

Crick was originally not a member of the club (nor was Watson). But he wrote some extremely important letters and papers to club members. One of these, entitled "On Degenerate Templates and the Adapter Hypothesis," contained the ideas described above.

Over the next half-dozen years, scientists began to collect information about adapter molecules. Crick had been correct again! Such molecules do exist in cells, and they work just as he had predicted they would. The molecules turned out to be another kind of ribonucleic acid. Eventually they became known by their modern name, transfer RNA, or tRNA.

In 1977, Crick left Cambridge University. He later explained that he felt he had worked long enough on nucleic acids and that he "wanted a new challenge." That challenge was brain research.

Crick's interest in neurobiology—the biology of the nervous system—went back to the 1940s. In fact, at the point that he decided to leave physics, he was uncertain as to whether he should turn his attention to "the borderline between the living and the nonliving, and the workings of the brain." He chose the former, he says, because his "existing scientific background would be more easily applied to the first problem."

Still, his interest in neurobiology never really disappeared. By 1977, the opportunity presented itself for Crick to turn his attention to new fields of research. He was invited to become Kieckhefer Distinguished Research Professor at the Salk Institute for Biological Studies in La Jolla, California.

Francis Crick and James Watson on the occasion of the 30th anniversary of the discovery of the DNA structure. (Cold Spring Harbor Laboratory)

To no one's surprise, Crick threw himself into his new topic with energy and enthusiasm. He began to familiarize himself with everything that had been done on brain research and to suggest new theories that might explain this research.

Eventually he decided to concentrate on the subject of dreams. In 1983 he published an important paper on this topic with Graeme Mitchison, a British mathematician. In this paper, Crick and Mitchison proposed a theory about the purpose of dreams.

Individuals in every human culture have tried to figure out what the meaning of dreams is. Some societies have believed that dreams are messages from the gods. Sigmund Freud, the father of modern psychoanalysis, thought that dreams reveal a whole hidden world of mental activity. He called dreams "the royal road to the unconscious."

Crick and Mitchison proposed a quite different meaning for dreams. Dreams are, they wrote, a way by which the brain forgets or "unlearns" useless information.

Think of all the information a human brain receives every day. The brain can hold only a certain amount of that information. Over a period of time, too much information can cause the brain to become cluttered and confused. Perhaps the way the brain deals with the problem, Crick and Mitchison said, is for it to do a "housecleaning" each night.

This "housecleaning" may occur during the period of sleep known as REM sleep. The term *REM* stands for rapid-eye-movement. During REM sleep, the brain is unusually active. A person who is awakened during REM sleep can usually remember dreams that were taking place at the time.

These dreams, Crick and Mitchison think, occur because the brain is sorting through its memory. It is deciding which memories to keep and which to "throw away," that is, to forget. Crick and Mitchison have also described this process as "reverse learning." The process of reverse learning supposedly leaves parts of the brain clean, fresh, and ready to record new memories during the next day.

Brain researchers agree that the Crick-Mitchison model explains many research findings about dreams. For example, babies experience twice as much REM sleep as do adults. Perhaps this means their brains have more "sorting out" and "organizing" to do than do the brains of adults.

Other researchers are less sure about the theory. One sleep expert has said that the Crick-Mitchison model is "interesting and worthy of publication and discussion," but he "personally doubt[s] that REM sleep evolved for reverse learning."

Everyone involved in brain research seems to agree on one point about the Crick-Mitchison theory. Testing the idea will be extraordinarily difficult. It will probably be a very long time before anyone knows if this is another of Crick's brilliant ideas or a clever detour along a blind alley. By the time that happens, one writer has predicted, Crick will "probably have moved on to a different field and another modest proposal" with which to startle the scientific community.

Another of Crick's later interests has been the subject of panspermia. The word panspermia means "seeds everywhere." The concept was first proposed by the Swedish chemist, Svante Arrhenius, in 1908. Arrhenius suggested that life originated somewhere else in the universe. Then, some types of spores escaped from this point of origin and traveled to the Earth. Here they took root, developed, and evolved into life as we know it.

Crick and Leslie Orgel, a biochemist at the Salk Institute, reintroduced that idea in the early 1980s. They suggested the theory that an advanced civilization in some other part of the universe consciously decided to send out seeds of life to Earth in a spaceship. They called their idea *directed panspermia*.

Crick explained the idea of directed panspermia in great detail in his 1981 book, *Life Itself: Its Origin and Nature*. He outlined existing scientific evidence that might support the idea of directed panspermia. For example, he pointed out that "sufficient time had elapsed [since the creation of the universe] for life to have evolved twice."

The book was not received enthusiastically by everyone. For example, Watson called it "monumentally silly." Some people were upset that Crick seemed to have slipped into writing science fiction. They thought that the idea of panspermia was fanciful, strange, and certainly scientifically unproductive.

Francis Crick at The Salk Institute in 1991.
(The Salk Institute)

But some of these critics had not looked closely enough at *Life Itself*. For in the book, Crick had also argued *against* the idea of directed panspermia. He reviewed the scientific evidence that could be used on both sides of the theory.

He later explained that his object in writing *Life Itself* was not so much to convince people of the truth of directed panspermia. It was, instead, to show how theories about the origin of life could and should be tested.

Nonetheless, Crick has had enough confidence in the idea of directed panspermia to suggest how humans might use the process today. He has outlined a method for launching bacteria in spaceships to uninhabited planets. "How ironic," he has said, "yet how fitting, that we who may be descended from space-borne spores should launch toward outer space 'directed panspermia' capsules containing billions of bacteria!"

Francis Crick has obviously not exhausted his innovative, creative, stimulating, and controversial ideas for the future of the world!

CHAPTER 6 NOTES

p. 74   "proteins can do . . ." Lois N. Magner, *A History of the Life Sciences* (New York: Marcel Dekker, 1979), p. 466.

p. 75   "is a simple code . . ." Horace Freeland Judson, *The Eighth Day of Creation* (New York: Simon and Schuster, 1979), p. 335.

p. 76   "He's just not . . ." Judson, *The Eighth Day*, p. 456.

p. 79   "but a multi-molecular . . ." Robert Olby, *The Path to the Double Helix* (Seattle: University of Washington Press, 1979), p. 433.

p. 79   "once 'information' has passed . . ." Olby, *Path*, pp. 432, 456.

p. 83   "to solve the riddle . . ." Judson, *The Eighth Day*, p. 265.

p. 83   "wanted a new challenge." As quoted in "Crick, Francis (Harry Compton)," *Current Biography Yearbook, 1983*, from an interview by Yorick Blumenfeld in *Geo* (July 1982): p. 70.

p. 84   "existing scientific . . ." Francis Crick, *What Mad Pursuit* (New York: Basic Books, 1988), p. 17.

p. 85   "the royal road . . ." Theodore Melnechuk, "The Dream Machine," *Psychology Today* (November 1983): p. 34.

p. 86   "is interesting . . ." Melnechuk, "The Dream Machine," p. 34.

p. 86   "probably have moved on . . ." Daniel Goleman, "Crick's Twitch," *Psychology Today* (August 1982): p. 80.

p. 86   "sufficient time . . ." Pamela Weintraub, "Sperm from deep space: Francis Crick," *The Omni Interviews* (New York: Ticknor & Fields, 1984), p. 28.

p. 86   "monumentally silly," Interview with James D. Watson,
         Omni (May 1984): p. 77
p. 87   "How ironic . . ." Francis Crick, "Seeding the universe,"
         Science Digest (November 1981): pp. 82–84+.

7

JAMES WATSON: THE LATER YEARS

What lay ahead for James Dewey Watson in the summer of 1953? He had already made a discovery that would assure his fame in science. He had conquered one of the most difficult and most important of all questions in biology. How could he ever top that achievement? Should he even try?

One possible line of research seemed obvious, not only to Watson, but also to everyone else interested in DNA. Even before the DNA puzzle had been solved, Watson had taped the following note above his desk:

DNA → RNA → proteins

Both he and Crick were convinced that the genetic code in DNA was somehow transferred to RNA. The RNA code was then used to make proteins. Perhaps the next problem was to solve the structure of RNA and discover its role in protein synthesis.

During his two-year stay at Cal Tech (1953–55), Watson devoted himself to this question. He tried to use the same methods on RNA that had worked so well with DNA. But the effort was not successful. X-ray photographs of RNA molecules proved to be much more difficult to obtain. And his efforts at model-building produced no new insights on RNA. Watson's research on RNA proved to be largely a dead end.

In the fall of 1955, Watson moved to Harvard University, where he became an assistant professor of biology. In addition to his teaching responsibilities, he continued to do research. His interests shifted from RNA to other topics, including cell growth, cell membranes, and bacteriophages. He was especially involved in the

James Watson at Cold Spring Harbor in the summer of 1953. (Cold Spring Harbor Laboratory Research Library Archives)

study of viruses and the way in which they turn normal cells into cancer cells.

Gradually, however, Watson began to spend less time on research and more time on teaching, administration, and writing. By the time he received his Nobel Prize in 1962, he had essentially abandoned research. In fact, he published only one more research paper after receiving the prize.

Opinions about Watson's qualities as a teacher have varied widely. Most students and colleagues agree that he was never an especially inspirational lecturer. They have compared his style to that of "a bumbling Jimmy Stewart, who talks to his shoes and mumbles at the blackboard in lectures." One observer has written that Watson "is said sometimes to give his students the impression that he is 'muttering into his shirt pocket.'"

Watson lecturing at Harvard University. (Cold Spring Harbor Laboratory Research Library Archives)

His manner with students has been described as bored and abrasive. One interviewer claims that Watson "sometimes seems to ignore his students completely, and he sometimes says things to them with such candor and frankness that they may be bruised for weeks." Another reporter has said that Watson can be so "blunt and even abrasive" that some of his students "told that they were doing useless work, have burst into tears."

Even colleagues and administrators have not escaped Watson's sharp criticisms. He has labeled those with whom he disagrees or of whom he disapproves "taxonomists." (A taxonomist is someone who classifies and names organisms.) To Watson's thinking, that would be the lowest position any biologist could hold.

On the other hand, both colleagues and students have always expressed the highest respect for Watson's intellectual skills, and many praise his ability to inspire students. One graduate student has remarked on Watson's "uncanny instinct for the important problem, the thing that leads to the big-time results."

Another student felt that Watson's confidence in himself and in his students was his most important quality. "You can work for a long time without success," he said, "and it's very important to have someone who'll keep telling you, 'I know this is right. Keep going.'" Watson does that.

This image of Watson-the-teacher matches the reports given of Watson-the-man. A towering intellect, he is absolutely committed to the pursuit of science. His one passion is the advancement of knowledge. One associate has said that "His dominant moral value is good science." He is not, however, overly troubled by social niceties. He says what he believes, without much concern as to who may be hurt.

By the early 1960s, Watson had turned his attention to another interest, writing. He completed his textbook, *The Molecular Biology of the Gene*, in 1965. It is now in its fourth edition and is widely recognized as a classic in the field.

His more famous book, however, is *The Double Helix*, begun in 1962. Watson decided that he wanted to write a book that would tell his version of how the DNA puzzle was solved. He worked on the manuscript, on and off, for the next four years. His original title for the book was "Honest Jim." The title referred to a nickname some colleagues had given him. It alluded to his somewhat unauthorized use of Rosalind Franklin's photograph 51.

In 1966, Watson sent copies of the first draft of "Honest Jim" to Crick, Wilkins, and a number of others who had been involved in the search for the double helix. Many of those who read the manuscript were outraged or upset. A few were probably offended by the way they were portrayed in the book. Some thought the book intruded on their privacy. Still others felt the book turned a great scientific story into cheap gossip. Others found the book too one-sided, presenting a story that was different from what they had remembered of events.

Crick himself wrote Watson that the manuscript was similar to "that found in the lower class of women's magazines." He was probably justified in being upset at the opening line of Watson's book: "I have never seen Francis Crick in a modest mood." Crick and Wilkins both refused to sign a release for the book. Reportedly, Crick may even have threatened to sue Watson if the manuscript ever actually appeared in print.

The depth of Crick's anger was revealed in an article he wrote for *Nature* in 1974. He admitted that he had considered the possibility of writing his own version of the DNA story. His tentative title was "The Loose Screw." About as far as he got was the catchy opening line: "Jim was always clumsy with his hands. One only had to see him peel an orange."

The reaction of his colleagues to the manuscript did not make Watson change his mind. After making a few changes in the text, he decided to go ahead with his publishing plans. However, his intended publisher, Harvard University Press, had different ideas. Harvard's president, Nathan Pusey, was upset at the reactions of Crick, Wilkins, and others. He did not want the university to become involved in a "trans-Atlantic argument among scientists." So he ordered the university press to drop plans to produce the book.

Watson's response was to offer the book to another publisher, Atheneum Press. Atheneum accepted the manuscript but did not have big plans for the book. It ordered an initial printing of only 7,500 copies. However, word of the controversy over Watson's book soon began to leak out. For example, Harvard's student newspaper, *The Crimson*, began writing about the "dirty book" that the university press had rejected. To Atheneum's surprise, the book became a great success. It remained on the *New York Times* best-seller list for 18 weeks in 1968.

Critics responded to *The Double Helix* in a variety of ways. Some were as offended by its gossipy style as were Crick and Wilkins. John Lear, the science editor of the *Saturday Review*, for example, called it a "bleak recitation of bickering and personal ambition." He was especially critical of Watson's treatment of Rosalind Franklin. He referred to it as an "attempt to bully a proud woman scientist into discussing details of her X-ray studies of DNA" and described Watson's "craven retreat from her laboratory when her anger rose."

Lear wrote that he was especially concerned about "the effect [the book] may have on immature minds . . . The more idealistic they are, the more they are needed in science, and the more negatively they will react to Watson's story of how one Nobel Prize was won."

Another participant in the DNA race, Erwin Chargaff, also took a dim view of the book. He predicted that "habitual readers of gossip columns will like the book immensely. . .They will be happy to hear all about the marital difficulties of one distinguished scientist (p. 26), the kissing habits of another (p. 66), or the stomach problems of a third (p. 136)."

Others, however, praised the book for showing readers the human side of science. For example, the eminent biologist, Jacob Bronowski, wrote that "the book communicates the spirit of science as no formal account has ever done . . . it will bring home to the non-scientist how the scientific method really works."

Also, Harvard professor Richard Lewontin said that the book showed the true competition and aggressive nature of science, "a contest of man against man that provides knowledge as a side product."

Eventually, most of those involved in the DNA story took a kindlier view toward *The Double Helix*. Crick himself has said that the book should be viewed "not really as history but as a fragment of Jim's autobiography. When you look at it that way, it takes on a different complexion." Although Crick and Watson once again became friendly, they never again collaborated and have had virtually no professional contact with each other.*

In any case, *The Double Helix* continues to be an enormous success. It has been translated into 17 languages and has been called "a modern classic." One reviewer has pointed out that Watson's book "not only made a lot of money; it created a genre." This new form of writing, he claims, helps readers learn more about science by learning more about the people who do science.

Over the last two decades, Watson has become, more than anything else, an administrator of science. In the process, he has become deeply involved in the politics of science: setting research goals, obtaining money for research projects, bringing scientists together to work on projects, lobbying Congress on behalf of scientific research, and so on.

Watson's interest in the political side of science goes back to his time at Harvard. During his years there he served in a variety of appointed positions, such as consultant to the President's Scientific Advisory Committee, member of a governmental project on biological warfare, and member of a boll-weevil eradication study group.

In 1968, Watson was presented with an opportunity to devote more time to administration and less to teaching. He accepted an appointment as unpaid director of the Cold Spring Harbor (CSH) laboratory. He continued to work at Harvard but now spent weekends and vacations at CSH. By 1976 he decided to make a full-time commitment to CSH and retired from his position as full professor at Harvard.

The Cold Spring Harbor position provided Watson with the chance to do one of the things he does best—bring researchers together in a setting where they can attack important biological problems. Scientists who come to CSH have no teaching or administrative duties. They are expected to concentrate entirely on their own research.

---

*The one notable exception was their reunion during the 30th anniversary celebration, in 1983, of the discovery of the double helix.

During Watson's time at CSH, a major topic of study was viruses and the cancers they cause in animals. He recruited some of the best scientists in the world to work on this problem, established a new laboratory for them to work in, and found the money they needed for their research.

Many scientists regard CSH as an almost perfect place to do their research. The laboratories there provide them with "almost total isolation" from the outside world. Dr. Alfred Hershey, a CSH scientist for well over three decades, says of the lab that "It is in the worst sense an ivory tower, but in a good sense it is what the world needs and isn't supplying any more."

Friends point out that the James Watson who directs the activities of Cold Spring Harbor is a different man from the James Watson seen almost anywhere else. There he is always willing to be "tactful, diplomatic, and gracious."

Nobel Prize winners at a meeting honoring the founding of the Laboratory of Molecular Biology in Cambridge in 1987. From left to right: Jim Watson, Max Perutz, Cesar Milstein, Fred Sanger, John Kendrew, Aaron Klug. (Medical Research Council Laboratory of Molecular Biology)

It seems clear that CSH is a very special place for Watson. It has been his professional and intellectual home for more than 30 years. He took the position as director, he pointed out, because "no one else was going to take over this place and keep it the way I thought it should be kept."

In 1988, James Watson turned 60. He had become one of the best-known, most widely respected biologists in the world. He had accomplished more in the fields of research, writing, and administration than most other scientists of his age. One could have excused him for taking a break, resting on his laurels, and retiring from the field of science.

But such was not to be. Instead, he took on yet another challenge. In 1988, he was offered the position of director of the Office of Human Genome Research at the National Institutes of Health (NIH). Watson accepted the challenge.

The Human Genome Project is a program designed to identify ("map") all the genes found in humans. The term human genome refers to all of the genes contained in human bodies. It is a project made possible originally by Watson and Crick's discovery of the structure of DNA.

Remember that Watson and Crick showed that the hereditary message in cells is stored in the nitrogen bases found in DNA. It is the exact sequence of bases that tells a cell which proteins it is supposed to manufacture. All of the physical attributes found in humans, therefore, are coded for in the base sequences of DNA molecules. Some biologists believe that these base sequences also code for other human attributes, such as intelligence, patriotism, motherly love, and the like. They would argue that every quality that can be considered "human" is somehow coded for in the bases of DNA molecules. A relatively new field of science, called sociobiology, is devoted to looking for the genetic basis of all human characteristics.

What the Watson-Crick discovery ultimately suggests is that it is theoretically possible to know everything about human characteristics by identifying the sequence of all nitrogen bases in all DNA molecules that occur in humans. Whether "everything about human characteristics" refers to a limited number of physical traits or to all human characteristics of any kind is still a matter of serious dispute

In any case, the actual research task that scientists face is clear. To understand the human genome completely, they will have to determine the sequence of the approximately 3 billion nitrogen bases that occur in human DNA.

Only a few years ago, that task would have seemed impossible. It was certainly a theoretical possibility, but the time required for the job appeared to be far too great for humans ever to accomplish. But then scientists invented machines that can "read" a DNA molecule and report the sequence of bases in the molecule. Maps of segments of the molecule can be produced in a matter of hours, rather than years. The task that had seemed impossible in 1980 had become not only possible but also very "doable" in 1990.

The genome project is still an incredibly difficult one. It will cost at least $3 billion and will involve thousands of scientists working in dozens of laboratories all around the world.

Watson's challenge is staggering. Some of the problems he faces are largely scientific and technological. New instruments for analyzing DNA will have to be developed. Computer programs for analyzing data will have to be written. New and existing data will have to be brought together and interpreted.

Other problems are administrative, similar to those he has faced at CSH. He will have to locate researchers, assign specific projects, and allocate the funds needed to keep the project on track.

Another challenge will be to deal with governmental bureaucracies. His NIH office is only one of many agencies involved in the overall genome project. The Energy Department, for example, also has a very large research center working on genome projects. Furthermore, research and financial support for the genome project is coming from other nations, such as the Soviet Union, France, and Japan.

Finally, Watson is having to deal with the difficult ethical issues created by the genome project. What will happen, some critics ask, when scientists do sequence the complete human genome? That accomplishment will allow scientists to cure genetic disorders, for example, a desirable goal. But it may also make it possible to "engineer" fetuses, to make babies with any characteristics people choose to give them.

Watson has been aware of the ethical dilemmas involved in genetic research for more than two decades. In 1971 he wrote an article published in *The Atlantic* discussing the ethical issues involved in altering human genes. As director of the NIH Human Genome Project, he has decided to allocate 3% of the project's budget to a study of the ethical implications of gene mapping.

Many critics of the genome project are pleased that Watson is giving the consideration of ethical issues an important place in the project. An example of the praise he has received for this decision is the remark of Dr. Maynard Olson, a member of the NIH Genome Advisory Board. Watson's action is, according to Dr. Olson, "a courageous and precedent-setting position to take."

The choice of Watson to lead the NIH genome office has pleased many of his colleagues. That is not to say, however, that he has mellowed or softened his manner of dealing with scientists, politicians, and the general public. In 1989, for example, Watson lashed out at the Japanese for contributing so little money to the genome project.

Watson noted that the Japanese were spending only $8 million a year on genome research, compared to the $90 million spent in the United States. Also, Japan had contributed nothing at all to the Human Genome Organization (HUGO), the coordinating agency for all genome research.

The problem, Watson pointed out, is that the Japanese will still have access to the results of gene research going on everywhere, including the United States. That research will be printed in scientific journals that anyone, including the Japanese, can read.

Watson's point was that "It is against the American national interest to work out the human genome and pass it out free to the rest of the world." He seemed to warn the Japanese that if they made no financial contributions to the project, they would not have access to U.S. findings. "I'm all for peace," he said, "but if there is going to be a war, I will fight it."

Many of Watson's colleagues were alarmed—but not especially surprised—at Watson's attack on the Japanese. James Watson has not really changed very much in his new job. He is still passionately committed to progress in science. And he is still willing to say exactly what he thinks, bluntly and directly.

In a recent interview with a writer for the *Smithsonian* magazine, Watson looked back on his childhood. He remembered that "I wasn't a popular kid, and I suspect it was because I would generally say something which I thought was true. In those days, I used to think manners were terrible, you know. The truth was important and manners often hid the truth." After 50 years of growing up, Watson has apparently not changed his mind on this point.

CHAPTER 7 NOTES

p. 92   "a bumbling Jimmy Stewart . . ." Lee Edson, "Says Nobelist James (Double Helix) Watson, 'To Hell with Being Discovered when You're Dead'," *New York Times Magazine* (October 19, 1962): p. 28.

p. 92   "is said sometimes to . . ." "Watson, a Quiz Kid and 'Child Prodigy,' Now 'Young Turk'," *New York Times* (October 19, 1962): p. 27.

p. 94   "sometimes seems to ignore . . ." Will Bradbury, "Genius on the prowl," *Life* (October 30, 1970): p. 62.

p. 94   "blunt and even abrasive . . ." Edson, "Says Nobelist," p. 28.

p. 94   "uncanny instinct . . . " Edson, "Says Nobelist," p. 29.

p. 94   "You can work . . ." Bradbury, "Genius," p. 62.

p. 94   "His dominant moral value . . ." Stephen S. Hall, "James Watson and the Search for Biology's 'Holy Grail,'" *Smithsonian* (February 1990): p. 42.

p. 95   "that found in . . ." Quoted in Horace Freeland Judson, *The Eighth Day of Creation* (New York: Simon and Schuster, 1979), p. 182.

p. 95   "Jim was always clumsy . . ." Francis Crick, "The Double Helix: A Personal View," *Nature* (April 26, 1974): p. 768.

p. 95   "trans-Atlantic argument . . ." Edson, "Says Nobelist," p. 44.

p. 96   "bleak recitation . . ." John Lear, "Hereditary Trans-actions," *Saturday Review* (March 16, 1968): p. 36.

p. 96   "the effect [the book] . . ." Lear, "Hereditary transactions," p. 86.

p. 96   "habitual readers . . ." Erwin Chargaff, "A Quick Climb up Mount Olympus," *Science* (March 29, 1968): p. 1448.

p. 96   "the book communicates . . ." Jacob Bronowski, "*The Double Helix*," *Nation* (March 18, 1968): p. 381.

p. 96   "a contest . . ." Lewontin's review appeared in the Chicago *Sun-Times*, as quoted in George Johnson, "Two Sides to Every Science Story," *New York Times Book Review* (April 9, 1989): p. 39.

p. 96   "not really as history . . ." in Pamela Weintraub, ed., "Sperm from deep space: Francis Crick," *The Omni Interviews* (New York: Ticknor & Fields, 1984), p. 23.

p. 97   "not only made a lot of money . . ." Johnson, "Two sides," p. 39.

p. 98   "It is in the worst sense . . ." Bradbury, "Genius," p. 60

p. 99   "no one else . . ." Bradbury, "Genius," p. 64.

p. 101   "a courageous . . ." Hall, "James Watson," p. 48.

p. 101   "It is against . . ." Leslie Roberts, "Watson versus Japan," *Science* (November 3, 1989): p. 576.

p. 101   "I'm all for peace . . ." Leslie Roberts, "Watson versus Japan," p. 576.

p. 102   "I wasn't a popular kid . . ." Hall, "James Watson," p. 43.

8

WHAT DOES IT ALL MEAN?

In *The Double Helix*, Watson describes Francis Crick's reaction when he realized they had solved the puzzle of DNA's structure. During a lunch break at the Eagle, Crick reportedly told "everyone within hearing distance that we had found the secret of life." Crick says he does not recall having made that remark. Whether he did or not, it turned out to be very close to the truth. At a very basic level, the structure of the DNA molecule does tell a great deal about the meaning of life.

Unraveling the mystery of the double helix has brought about a revolution in biology. Scientists now have a completely new way of thinking about living organisms. The goal of using chemistry and physics to understand life—expressed by Crick in his 1947 Medical Research Council application—has been attained. The science that has grown up as a result of discoveries like that of Watson and Crick is now known as molecular biology.

One result of the Watson-Crick revolution has been a philosoph-ical change in the way that life can be viewed. A half-century ago, most people would probably have agreed that living things possess some special quality that sets them apart from nonliving things. That quality might be called a "vital spirit," as described in the Introduction, "the breath of God," or some other mysterious or supernatural force.

Crick and Watson have shown that another view of life is possible. The special attributes of life—whether one is talking about a cabbage, an amoeba, a badger, or a human—can be explained in terms of atoms and molecules. One no longer needs to call on spirits and gods to explain the fact that one has blonde hair and green eyes and is left-handed. Scientists now know that these qualities, and untold numbers of other human traits, are the result of the way nitrogen bases are arranged along DNA molecules in the cells of one's body.

That discovery can dramatically change the way a person views the world. One benefit of any scientific discovery is that it makes nature less mysterious and more understandable. Few people today think that rainfall depends on the acts of rain spirits or rain gods. Most people have abandoned the notion that earthquakes are acts of punishment given out by angry supernatural beings. Few farmers depend on human sacrifices to assure that crops will grow well.

These notions stretch back to a time when nature was not well understood. Rainfall, earthquakes, and plant growth were thought to depend on the whims of gods and spirits. Humans could never know what to expect from an unpredictable and often frightening natural world.

Science has shown that each of these natural events has a cause that can be understood. Sometimes this understanding can lead to a new ability to control the events of nature. Today, for example, farmers have many methods for controlling plant growth. In other cases, people are only beginning to find ways to control natural events. Some people have been able to make changes in the amount of rain that falls. And in some cases— earthquakes are an example—human understanding of nature will probably never lead to control, although prediction may well be possible.

The important point is that an improved understanding of the causes of natural events allows humans to have more control over their own lives. They can feel less at the mercy of mysterious, unknown, supernatural forces. The Watson-Crick discovery extends human understanding of nature and one's sense of self-confidence to the most important part of the natural world, that of life itself.

Unraveling the DNA puzzle has had many important practical consequences also. These practical results depend on one basic principle: If the characteristics of living things are determined by the structure of a chemical molecule, then those characteristics can

be altered by making changes in that molecule. The process in-
volves nothing other than physical and chemical techniques that
are already known or that can eventually be developed.

Consider the example of genetic disorders. Accidents sometimes
occur within a cell that change the sequence of bases on a DNA
molecule. For example, radiation can knock a nitrogen base completely off a DNA molecule. The loss of just one base can change
the code stored in that molecule.

For example, suppose that the starred base (*) is lost from the
base sequence shown below.

$-D-P-D-P-D-P-D-P-D-P-D-P-D-P-D-P-D-$

| | | | | | | | |

C   T   C   A   C*   G   C   T   T

Before the loss of the base, the sequence above would transcribe
into the mRNA sequence shown below.

$-R-P-R-P-R-P-R-P-R-P-R-P-R-P-R-P-R-$

| | | | | | | | |

G   A   G   U   G   C   G   A   A

―――――――――   ―――――――――   ―――――――――

    codon 1   codon 2   codon 3

This sequence translates into the sequence of amino acids

― glutamic acid   ―   cysteine   ―   glutamic acid ―
   (from codon 1)   (from codon 2)   (from codon 3)

But look at the sequence of bases in DNA if the starred base is
lost:

$-D-P-D-P-D-P-D-P-D-P-D-P-D-P-D-P-D-$

| | | | | | | |

C   T   C   A   G   C   T   T

The mRNA sequence produced by this DNA molecule will be different. It will have the form:

$-$ R $-$ P $-$ R $-$ P $-$ R $-$ P $-$ R $-$ P $-$ R $-$ P $-$ R $-$ P $-$ R $-$ P $-$ R $-$

| | | | | | | |

G   A   G   U   C   G   A   A

     codon 1   codon 2   codon 3

The first codon (GAG) is the same as before. But the second codon is now UCG, rather than UGC. The new codon (UCG) codes for a different amino acid (serine) than does the old one (UGC). The same is likely to be true for codon 3, codon 4, and every other codon that follows. The loss of a single nitrogen base on the DNA molecule produces a whole new, different, and incorrect genetic code.

This kind of change is known as a *mutation*. Mutations occur when a nitrogen base is lost from, added to, or changed in a nucleic acid. Mutations often produce disastrous results for an organism. Suppose that the original, correct code given above tells a cell how to make the hemoglobin protein. Hemoglobin is the substance in blood that carries oxygen to the cells.

The altered code produced by the mutation will probably carry the wrong instructions for making hemoglobin. In one case, the message might make no sense to the cell at all. The cell will make no hemoglobin molecules at all. Or the cell might make incorrect forms of the hemoglobin molecule. In either case, the person's blood will not carry oxygen to cells as efficiently as it should. One medical condition produced by mutations in the hemoglobin molecule is *sickle-cell anemia*. A person with sickle-cell anemia is likely to become ill and, perhaps, to die.

Sometimes babies are born with DNA that has been damaged by mutations. When that happens, the baby may become ill immediately or later in life. Problems resulting from damaged DNA are classified as *genetic disorders*. Sickle-cell anemia, hemophilia, muscular dystrophy, diabetes, Tay-Sachs disease, Huntington's disease, and spina bifida are a few examples of genetic disorders.

Scientists think that at least 3,000 different medical conditions may be the result of damaged DNA.

Knowing the chemical structure of DNA molecules provides a way of dealing with genetic disorders. Suppose scientists discover, for example, that a particular kind of genetic disorder is caused by a mutation like the one described above: A cytosine base is lost from one part of a DNA molecule. One way to prevent that disorder, then, is to repair the damaged DNA molecule. By inserting a cytosine base where it belongs in the molecule, the DNA will be restored to its proper form.

The basic idea involved is simple, but the practice is not. The approach that scientists take is this. They make up many copies of a correct DNA molecule in the laboratory. Then they insert these correct DNA molecules into the cells of a person who has the genetic disorder. The best time to do this is before the person is born, when it is still a fetus in its mother's womb. With luck, the cell begins to read the code on the inserted DNA. It begins to make the correct molecules. Experiments of this kind are known as human gene therapy (HGT).

Many scientists are now working on this technique. They are trying to find the most effective ways of inserting new DNA into cells. They are looking for ways to get the new DNA to work properly—to "be expressed"—in cells.

The first attempt to use human gene therapy with a human being was made in September 1990. It was performed on a four-year-old girl with severe combined immunodeficiency disorder (SCID). SCID is a disorder in which a person's immune system completely fails. The body is unable to fight off any kind of infection.

A person with SCID normally does not live very long. He or she may die from even the simplest infection that would be no more than an inconvenience for other people. One way to protect SCID patients from infections is to have them live inside a large plastic bubble. The bubble prevents the person from coming into contact with the germs that could kill him or her. That kind of life is very expensive and very unpleasant, however.

The purpose of the 1990 experiment was to give this four-year-old girl a new set of altered DNA molecules. These molecules carried the correct genetic code for providing immunity. If the experiment works, the girl's cells will begin to read the inserted DNA molecules. They will begin to provide the immunity she does not now have.

Watson's current job with the Human Genome Project will contribute to this kind of research. Human gene therapy depends on knowing what the correct sequence of bases in DNA is. The first HGT trial in 1990, for example, could be done only because scientists had already discovered the proper base sequence for one part of DNA, the part that codes for this type of immunity.

If the same kind of HGT procedure is to be used for other genetic disorders, scientists must discover the correct base sequence in all DNA molecules in the human body. Thus, curing genetic disorders is one of the first and primary practical goals for information gained from the genome project. When that happens, one of the greatest promises of the 1953 Watson-Crick discovery will have been achieved.

The technique used in human gene therapy has many other applications. Many of these applications have already been tried; many are already in use. Consider the manufacture of human insulin as an example.

Diabetes is one of the most common of all genetic disorders. People with diabetes lack a substance—insulin—that allows their bodies to use the sugars they eat. By injecting insulin into their bodies on a regular basis, every day of their lives, diabetics can avoid the worst symptoms of diabetes and live a normal life.

Until recently, however, insulin was quite expensive. It could be obtained only from slaughtered animals. Today it is manufactured by recombinant DNA (rDNA) techniques. Here is how rDNA methods work.

Scientists make a fragment of DNA with the correct base sequence for some characteristic. For example, they can make a segment of DNA that has exactly the right base code for making insulin. This DNA segment is then attached to another molecule and inserted into bacterial cells. The synthetic DNA and the bacteria's own natural DNA are then "recombined" to make new DNA.

The bacteria are then placed in a large warm tank. They are given all the food they need. As the bacteria grow, they make all the chemicals that bacteria normally make when they are alive and

The method by which insulin can be produced by recombinant DNA procedures. (World Health Organization)

healthy. Plus, they make one more chemical—insulin. They make insulin because the code for doing so has been inserted into their DNA molecules.

All that needs to be done now is to remove the insulin from the vats containing the bacteria. Insulin made by this method is much less expensive than it is when taken from slaughtered animals.

The techniques of HGT and rDNA can, in theory, be applied to any organism. Scientists have already used these techniques on many different organisms, for many different purposes. For example, they have:

1. altered the segment of DNA in cows that controls milk production. Cows who received this form of DNA give a much greater amount of milk each day.
2. inserted altered forms of the DNA that control growth into humans who lack this DNA or who have a defective form of it. Children whose growth has been less than normal and who receive the DNA begin to grow to a more normal height.

3. modified the DNA in certain kinds of crops so that they will
   not be killed by herbicides (chemicals that normally kill plants).
   This procedure allows a farmer to use herbicides on a farm to
   kill weeds without harming the treated crops themselves.

Dozens of similar examples could be mentioned. The important
point is that scientists now have a method for altering the very
basic nature of life—of bacteria, wheat, cows, or humans. These
changes were all made possible by the Watson-Crick discovery of
the structure and function of DNA in 1953 and the discoveries in
the years that followed.

Some people are very concerned about the potential of this kind
of research. They ask whether humans have any right to change
the basic structure of plants, animals, and humans. They suggest
that by altering DNA molecules humans are "acting like God."

Most people probably agree that such research is a good idea in
some situations, as in the cure of genetic disorders. But they are
less certain about other applications. For example, should parents
really have the choice of deciding what color hair and eyes their
babies are going to have? The basic techniques for making this kind
of change are not really very much different from those used in
curing genetic disorders.

Having to deal with issues like these is one of the prices that
humans pay for knowing more about the natural world. Scientific
progress leaves people with less to fear about unknown, mysterious, supernatural forces, but it presents them with more choices
about the ways in which they want to live their lives and how they
want to deal with the natural world around them.

In reflecting on the dilemma over rDNA research, Watson has
written that risks and choices are an integral part of scientific
progress. "The future," he has pointed out, "automatically entails
risks and uncertainties."

In 1984, another Nobel Prize winner, David Baltimore, looked
back 30 years to the discovery of the structure of DNA. He reviewed
the potential benefits and risks to the world of that discovery. He
agreed that concern about the potential applications of human
gene therapy and recombinant DNA research was understandable.
But, he concluded, humans should "prepare as well as we can to

integrate the techniques of the future into our lives. It is," he said, "one of the most challenging areas of inquiry we can undertake."

CHAPTER 8 NOTES

p. 105   "everyone within hearing . . ." James Watson, *The Double Helix* (New York: Atheneum, 1968), p. 197

p. 112   "The future . . ." J. D. Watson, "In defense of DNA," *The New Republic* (June 25, 1977): p. 12.

pp. 112–113 "prepare as well as we can . . ." David Baltimore, "The brain of a cell," *Science* (November 1984): p. 151.

GLOSSARY

adapter molecule: *See* tRNA.

adenine: One of the nitrogen bases that occurs in nucleic acids.

amino acids: Organic compounds that contain two characteristic chemical groupings, the amino group (-NH2) and carboxyl (-COOH) group. Amino acids are the units of which proteins are made.

anaphase: the third stage in mitosis.

angstrom: A unit of measure equal to 10^{-10} meter or about 4×10^{-9} inch.

atom: The smallest part of an element that can exist and still retain all the properties of the element.

bacteriophages: Viruses that attack bacteria.

base: A class of chemical compounds all of which have similar physical and chemical characteristics. The bases that occur in nucleic acid molecules are a special type of the general class of compounds that contain nitrogen. (*See also* nitrogen base.)

base pairing: The process that occurs in nucleic acids in which a purine-type base pairs with a pyrimidine-type base.

biochemistry: The study of chemical compounds that occur in living organisms.

biology: The study of living organisms.

biophysics: That field of science concerned with the study of the physical characteristics of living organisms.

bonding: A general term that refers to any process by which two or more atoms are held together in chemical combination.

capsid: The protein shell that encloses the nucleic acid in a virus.

Central Dogma: The theory that genetic information passes from DNA to RNA to proteins in cells.

chemistry: The study of matter, its composition, and the changes that it undergoes.

chromosome: Long, rodlike particles in the nucleus of a cell that carry genetic information. Chromosomes are now known to consist of nucleic acids surrounded by protein coats.

codon: A sequence of three nitrogen bases in an mRNA molecule that corresponds to a particular amino acid.

covalent bond: A type of chemical bond consisting of a pair of electrons shared between two atoms.

crystallographer: A scientist who studies the structure of crystals.

cytosine: One of the nitrogen bases that occurs in nucleic acids.

deoxyribonucleic acid (DNA): A biochemical compound that consists of many nucleotides joined to each other and that carries the genetic information stored in cells.

deoxyribose: A type of pentose. (*See also* pentose.)

DNA: *See* deoxyribonucleic acid.

double helix: A pair of helices, intertwined with each other.

gene: A unit that carries hereditary information in cells. A gene is now known to correspond to a sequence of bases in a DNA molecule.

genetic code: A system by which sets of three nitrogen bases code for specific amino acids during the synthesis of proteins in cells.

genetic disorder: Any medical disability that arises when a person's body is unable to manufacture a particular compound necessary for good health and normal growth.

genetic engineering: *See* recombinant DNA.

genetics: The science that deals with the way in which hereditary characteristics are transmitted from one generation to the next.

genome: All of the genes contained in an organism's body.

guanine: One of the nitrogen bases that occurs in nucleic acids.

helix: A geometrical pattern with the shape of a coil.

hemoglobin: The molecule in red blood cells that carries oxygen to the cells.

host cell: Any cell that is infected by a foreign organism, such as a bacterium or virus, or into which is inserted some foreign material.

human gene therapy: Any type of medical procedure that attempts to prevent or cure some genetic disorder by changing the structure of DNA molecules in a person's body.

hydrogen bonding: The force between two molecules or two parts of a molecule that results from the weak electrical attraction between a partially positive charge on one and a partially negative charge on the other.

jig: Any kind of mechanical device used in the construction of models.

messenger RNA (mRNA): An RNA molecule that is produced according to a specific nitrogen base sequence in DNA and which then uses that sequence to direct the synthesis of a protein molecule.

metallic bond: A type of chemical bond in which a great many electrons are shared among a great many positively charged metallic ions.

metaphase: The second stage of mitosis.

microbiology: The biological study of microorganisms.

mitosis: The process of cell division.

molecular biology: That field of science in which biological phenomena are interpreted in terms of chemical and physical principles.

mutation: Any change in the base sequence of a DNA or RNA molecule.

neurobiology: The study of nerve cells and the nervous system.

nitrogen base: An organic compound consisting of a single- or double-ring compound that contains at least one nitrogen atom. The five nitrogen bases that occur in nucleic acids are adenine, cytosine, guanine, thymine, and uracil.

nucleic acid: A large, complex biochemical compound whose basic components are a sugar (ribose or deoxyribose), a phosphate group, and a nitrogen base.

nuclein: The original name for nucleic acid.

nucleotide: A chemical compound consisting of a nitrogen base and sugar joined to a phosphate group.

panspermia: A theory that life originated elsewhere in the universe than on Earth.

pentose: Any sugar that contains five carbon atoms. The two pentoses that occur in nucleic acid are ribose and deoxyribose.

phages: *See* bacteriophages.

phosphate group: A grouping of atoms consisting of one phosphorus atom to which are joined four oxygen atoms.

polynucleotide: Many nucleotides joined to each other. A nucleic acid is a very large polynucleotide.

polypeptide: A large molecule consisting of many amino acids joined to each other. Proteins are large polypeptides.

primary structure (of proteins): The sequence of amino acids that make up any particular protein molecule.

prophase: The first stage of mitosis.

protein: A large polypeptide. (*See also* polypeptide). Proteins carry out a number of important biological functions in an organism.

protein synthesis: The process by which new protein molecules are manufactured on ribosomes in a cell.

purine: A chemical compound containing nitrogen and consisting of two rings joined to each other. Cytosine, thymine and uracil have structures similar to that of purine.

pyrimidine: A chemical compound containing nitrogen and consisting of a single ring. Adenine and guanine have structures similar to that of pyrimidine.

recombinant DNA (rDNA): The transfer of a segment of the DNA from one organism to the DNA of a second organism by laboratory means.

reductionism: The concept that complex biological events and phenomena can be completely explained in terms of fundamental chemical and physical laws.

REM sleep: Rapid-eye-movement, a stage of normal sleep.

repeat distance (in a DNA molecule): The vertical distance required for one complete turn of the helix.

replication: The process by which a DNA molecule duplicates itself. The term also applies to mitosis.

ribonucleic acid (RNA): A class of biochemical compounds that consist of nucleotides containing the sugar ribose.

ribose: A type of pentose. (*See also* pentose.)

ribosome: Small structures in the cytoplasm of cells where protein synthesis takes place.

RNA: *See* ribonucleic acid.

secondary structure (of a protein): The three-dimensional shape (such as a helix) taken by a chain of amino acids that make up a protein.

sickle-cell anemia: A genetic disorder that results when a person's body does not carry the gene necessary to make a correct copy of the hemoglobin molecule.

sociobiology: A field of science that is devoted to looking for the genetic basis of all human characteristics.

sugar: A simple carbohydrate. Many different types of sugar exist. Those found in nucleic acid are ring compounds that contain five carbon atoms and are known as pentoses.

taxonomist: A scientist who classifies and names organisms.

telophase: The fourth stage of mitosis.

template: A pattern.

tertiary structure (of a protein): A higher order of three-dimensional shape taken by a protein, resulting from the twisting and bending of the molecule beyond that expressed by the secondary structure.

tetranucleotide hypothesis: A now abandoned theory that the structure of nucleic acids was quite simple, with the nitrogen bases arranged in a regular, repetitive pattern along the sugar-phosphate backbone.

thymine: A nitrogen base that occurs in DNA but not in RNA.

transcription: The process by which the genetic code stored in a DNA molecule is transferred to a newly formed mRNA molecule in the nucleus of a cell.

transfer RNA (tRNA): Molecules that collect amino acids from raw materials available in the cell and then transfer those amino acids to mRNA molecules on ribosomes during protein synthesis.

translation: The name given to the process by which the genetic message encoded in mRNA molecules is used to synthesize new protein molecules.

triple helix: Three helices, intertwined with each other.

uracil: A nitrogen base that occurs in RNA but not in DNA.

vector: Any substance or organism that is used to insert a fragment of DNA into a host cell during recombinant DNA processes.

virus: A particle, consisting of nucleic acid surrounded by a protein coat, responsible for many types of infections.

vitalism: A theory that living organisms are different from nonliving materials in some fundamental way.

X-ray crystallography: A method for studying the composition of materials by bombarding them with X rays and then interpreting the photograph produced by the reflection of those X rays.

FURTHER READING

Two brilliant books dealing with the discovery of the double helix have been written. Both are fairly advanced and may be difficult for the average teenager to read. However, both contain enough interesting information to make the effort worthwhile. The first is

Judson, Horace Freeland. *The Eighth Day of Creation*. New York: Simon and Schuster, 1979. This book goes far beyond the DNA story and is a bit more chatty than is the second book,

Olby, Robert. *The Path to the Double Helix*. Seattle: University of Washington Press, 1974. Olby's book contains more of the science involved in this story and is more difficult to read. Readers may be interested in a segment of the Olby book, written as an article for a scholarly journal, *Daedalus* (Olby, Robert, "Francis Crick, DNA, and the Central Dogma," *Daedalus*, Fall 1970).

Another book that devotes a fair amount of space to the Watson-Crick story but that also provides a lot of introductory and follow-up information is

Gribbin, John. *In Search of the Double Helix*. Aldershot, England: Wildwood House, 1985.

Books on the history of science and the history of biology provide a greater or lesser description of the search for the structure of DNA. One of the best of these is

Magner, Lois N. *A History of the Life Sciences*. New York: Marcel Dekker, 1979.

The biography of Rosalind Franklin not only provides a valuable story about this important scientist, but also gives another view of the search for the DNA structure.

Sayre, Anne. *Rosalind Franklin and DNA*. New York: Norton, 1975.

Each of the major characters in this story, Watson and Crick, has written his own account of the discovery of the DNA structure. Watson's is more famous, partly because it has now been in print for more than 20 years and partly because it is so well written and such a delight to read. Although he sneaks in a lot of science without the reader's knowing it, there is no danger that he or she will be distracted by the gossip for which the book is famous:

Watson, James D. *The Double Helix*. New York: Atheneum, 1968.

Francis Crick's own story of the hunt for DNA was published only in 1988. It tends to concentrate more on the science of the story and less on the personalities of those involved. The opening chapter that tells of Crick's youth is beautifully and interestingly written:

Crick, Francis. *What Mad Pursuit*. New York: Basic Books, 1988.

Crick has also written two other books describing his thoughts on vitalism and directed panspermia.

Crick, Francis. *Life Itself: Its Origin and Nature*. New York: Simon and Schuster, 1981.
Crick, Francis. *Of Molecules and Men*. Seattle: University of Washington Press, 1966.

Crick has also written articles that look back on the discovery of the DNA structure.

Crick, Francis, "How to Live with a Golden Helix," *The Sciences*, September 1979, 6–9.
Crick, Francis, "The Double Helix: A Personal View," *Nature*, April 26, 1974, 766–69.

Crick has also written a number of technical, semi-technical, and popular articles dealing with DNA and other topics in which he has been interested.

Crick, F. H. C., "The Genetic Code," *Scientific American*, October 1962, 66–72.

Crick, F. H. C., "The Genetic Code III," *Scientific American*, October 1966, 55–60.

Crick, F. H. C., "Nucleic Acids," *Scientific American*, May 1957, 188–192.

Crick, F. H. C., "Seeding the Universe," *Science Digest*, November 1981, 82–84+.

Crick, F. H. C., "The Structure of the Hereditary Material," *Scientific American*, October 1954, 54–61.

Crick, F. H. C., "Thinking about the Brain," *Scientific American*, September 1979, 219–32.

A number of articles by and about Watson have dealt with political, social, and ethical issues surrounding the practical uses of DNA research. Included among these are the following.

Roberts, Leslie, "Watson versus Japan," *Science*, November 3, 1989, 576–78.

Watson, J. D., "The Cancer Conquerors," *The New Republic*, February 26, 1972, 17–21.

Watson, James D., "DNA Folly Continues," *The New Republic*, January 13, 1979, 12+.

Watson, J. D., "Growing Up in the Phage Group," in John Cairns, Gunther S. Stent, and James D. Watson. *Phage and the Origins of Molecular Biology*. Cold Spring Harbor: Cold Spring Harbor Laboratory of Quantitative Biology, 1966; 239–45.

Watson, James D., "The Human Genome Project: Past, Present, and Future," *Science*, April 6, 1990, 44–48.

Watson, James D., "An Imaginary Monster," *Bulletin of the Atomic Scientists*, May 1977, 12–13.

Watson, J. D., "In Defense of DNA," *The New Republic*, June 25, 1977, 11–14.

Wright, Robert, "Achilles' Helix," *The New Republic*, July 9 & 16, 1990, 21–29.

Both Watson and Crick have been interviewed for major newspapers and magazines. These interviews provide some insight to what these men are like and what kind of work they have been and are now doing. The most important of these articles include:

Bradbury, Will, "Genius on the Prowl," *Life*, October 30, 1970, 57–60+.

Campbell, Neil A., "Discoverer of the Double Helix," *BioScience*, December 1986, 728–31.

Edson, Lee, "Says Nobelist James (Double Helix) Watson, 'To Hell with Being Discovered when You're Dead,'" *New York Times Magazine*, August 18, 1968, 26–27+.

Hall, Stephen S., "James Watson and the Search for Biology's 'Holy Grail,'" *Smithsonian*, February 1990, 40–49.

Interview with James D. Watson, *Omni*, May 1984, 74–77.

Weintraub, Pamela, Ed., "Sperm from Deep Space: Francis Crick," in *The Omni Interviews*. New York: Ticknor & Fields, 1984.

The only easily available interview with Wilkins is:

Johnson, Stephanie, and Thomas R. Mertens, "An Interview with Nobel Laureate Maurice Wilkins," *American Biology Teacher*, March 1989, 151–53.

A number of articles have been written about Watson and Crick and their work and ideas. Among the most important of these are the following:

Baltimore, David, "The Brain of a Cell," *Science 84*, November 1984, 149–51.

"Crick, Francis (Harry Compton)," *Current Biography Yearbook, 1983*. New York: H. W. Wilson, 1983; 68–71.

Frazier, Kendrick, "Twists in the Double Helix," *Science News*, June 15, 1974, 388–90.

Goleman, Daniel, "Crick's Twitch," *Psychology Today*, August 1982, 80.

Johnson, George, "Two Sides to Every Story," *New York Times Book Review*, April 9, 1989, 1+.

Melnechuk, Theodore, "The Dream Machine," *Psychology Today*, November 1983, 22–27+.

Mirsky, Alfred, "The Discovery of DNA," *Scientific American*, June 1968, 78–84+.

"Watson, James Dewey," *Current Biography Yearbook, 1963*. New York: H. W. Wilson, 1963, 458–60.

There is also some value in reading reviews of Watson's *The Double Helix* and of Sayre's *Rosalind Franklin and DNA*. Some of the most interesting are the following:

Bronowski, Jacob, "The Double Helix," *Nation*, March 18, 1968, 381–382.

Chargaff, Erwin, "A Quick Climb up Mount Olympus," *Science*, March 29, 1968, 1448–49.

Lear, John, "Heredity Transactions," *Saturday Review*, March 16, 1968, 36+.

Lwoff, Andre, "Truth, Truth, What Is Truth (About How the Structure of DNA Was Discovered)?" *Scientific American*, July 1968, 133–38.

Rabinowitch, Eugene, "The Double Helix," *Bulletin of the Atomic Scientists*, December 1968, 27–28.

Snow, C. P., "The Corridors of DNA," *New York Review of Books*, November 13, 1975, 3–4.

INDEX

Italic numbers indicate illustrations